The Final Curtain
Celebrity Deaths

Catherine Olen

4880 Lower Valley Road, Atglen, Pennsylvania 19310

Copyright © 2010 by Catherine Olen
*Unless otherwise noted all photos are the
property of the author.
 Library of Congress Control Number:
  2010920276

Designed by "Sue"
Type set in Demon/NewBskvll BT

ISBN: 978-0-7643-3472-6
Printed in the United States of America

Schiffer Books are available at special
discounts for bulk purchases for sales
promotions or premiums. Special editions,
including personalized covers, corporate
imprints, and excerpts can be created in
large quantities for special needs. For more
information contact the publisher:

Published by Schiffer Publishing Ltd.
4880 Lower Valley Road
Atglen, PA 19310
Phone: (610) 593-1777;
Fax: (610) 593-2002
E-mail: Info@schifferbooks.com

For the largest selection of fine
reference books on this and related
subjects, please visit our web site at:
www.schifferbooks.com
We are always looking for people to
write books on new and related subjects.
If you have an idea for a book please
contact us at the above address.

This book may be purchased from the
publisher. Include $5.00 for shipping.
Please try your bookstore first.
You may write for a free catalog.

In Europe, Schiffer books
are distributed by
Bushwood Books
6 Marksbury Ave.
Kew Gardens
Surrey TW9 4JF England
Phone: 44 (0) 20 8392 8585;
Fax: 44 (0) 20 8392 9876
E-mail: info@bushwoodbooks.co.uk
Website: www.bushwoodbooks.co.uk

CONTENTS

Above:
This broadview image of the cemetery of Hollywood Forever shows the grave of actor Darren McGavin and other impressive headstones.

DEDICATION

This book is lovingly dedicated to my husband Jeff, for his unending love and support in my obsession with celebrity grave hunting, and my daughter Brooke, for her patience and hours of assistance trekking through cemeteries to find the next gravesite.

INTRODUCTION

I can recall the date of June 25, 2009 clearly. It started with the announcement of the long expected death of 1970s icon Farrah Fawcett. It was sad, but not unexpected, as I had watched over the months the reports about her struggle for life against cancer and ultimate demise.

When the phone rang at noon, the voice on the other end was that of my twelve-year-old daughter calling from Indiana.

"Did you hear about Michael Jackson?" she asked.

"No, is he in trouble again?"

"No, he's dead. They say it's an overdose of pain medication."

I sat silently, struggling to come to grips with the fact that another celebrity life had been cut short. Just one more name on a long list of famous personalities who had been prescribed a laundry list of pain killers and sedatives to help them deal with their lives...and ultimately ending it too soon.

This death struck close to home for me as I thought about my childhood years watching Jackson and his brothers on television. The vibrant young performer captivating audiences with his voice and flowing dance moves. A seemingly gentle soul then...before the focus of his life shifted from the unending string of musical hits to the increasingly bizarre behavior that made headlines over the years.

Over the next few weeks, I took a front row seat, along with the rest of America, to say a lengthy goodbye to one of the most revered pop icons in recorded history. Numerous ceremonies took place across the United States. The main focus was on the public memorial in Los Angeles and where Jackson would ultimately be buried. Finally, a private burial at Forest Lawn in Glendale, California, seventy-one days after the pop star's death, closed the final chapter. The private family mausoleum is strictly off limits to the public and fierce security makes sure no one gets in to see Jackson since his final interment.

Who am I and why is this of particular interest to me? Well, I am in the business of dead celebrities and their final resting places. I'm a professional grave hunter. No, not gravedigger... *grave hunter*.

I started my grave hunting during my tenure working in the funeral industry in 1991. So many times I would be called to escort someone to the gravesite of one of our local celebrities here in the

The author is standing in front of the Warner Brothers crypt at Home of Peace Cemetery in Los Angeles.

Orange County area. Once we would arrive at the site, I would disappear so the visitor could have their time to memorialize a life that had touched them.

One day, I began thinking about the lives that had touched me and where the final resting places of these people might be. This being before the birth of the Internet as we know it today, my search took on a life of its own as the information was not readily available; it was mostly by word of mouth to find the gravesites of the celebrities I adored.

I suppose it really began when I stood at the gravesite of Walt Disney. If I hadn't been looking for his grave, I would have walked right past it, never knowing that such a great American was resting inches from where I stood. With reverence I walked into the small family plot and looked at the beautiful statue of a small girl adorning the lawn. I looked up and there it was — the simple, modest marker with the name Walter Elias Disney standing before me on the wall at eye level. It was a surreal experience as I found myself unable to move forward. Here lies the man who created all of my favorite childhood films and the Happiest Place on Earth, Disneyland. My happy place!

It took several minutes before I could compose myself enough to move forward and place a small bouquet of flowers at the base of the wall underneath his marker. I stood for a few moments more, reflecting on the life that was no longer with us. This modest man created a place where parents and children could enjoy their time together; a fantasyland where the troubles of the world could be left behind and you could enter the world of today, tomorrow, and fantasy, just as the bronze plaque at the entrance to Disneyland states. The same man, who created one of our most beloved characters, Mickey Mouse, would make a living creating simple children cartoons and the first full-length feature animated film of the time.

He didn't want awards or pats on the back; he just wanted people to enjoy his work and hoped it would live on in his absence. Little did we dream that on December 15, 1966, he would lose the battle with lung cancer and leave us with a legacy that would live on and touch generations long into the future. No fancy funeral, no elaborate tomb...just a simple garden where one could come and pay their respects with reverence and humility.

In the days and weeks that followed, my thirst for finding the final resting places of my favorite celebrities became insatiable. I bought books and looked up information on the web on all my favorite stars. I began haunting the cemeteries in Los Angeles and Hollywood, paying my respects to all the great lives that had touched not only me, but also many others. I found myself meeting a small group of people who found these places comforting and frequented them like others visit local parks.

This book — and the lives it contains — is my small way of memorializing these people and keeping their memories alive (no pun intended). Here's to the actors, actresses, directors, and producers who have touched us so deeply... May you rest in peace.

Chapter One:

EARLY HOLLYWOOD AND SUICIDE

It seems there is no end of movie stars deciding on an early curtain call to their life. Milton Sills ran his car off of Dead Man's Curve on Sunset Boulevard. Jeanne Eagels overdosed on heroin, and Karl Dane put a gun to his head. It seems that people have always been fascinated with celebrities and movie stars who die by their own hand. Here are just a few of the more notable ones.

PAUL BERN

One particularly well-publicized suicide was that of Paul Bern, the awarding-winning producer of "Grand Hotel." Bern's body was found in the nude September 5, 1932, a scant two months after he married actress Jean Harlow on July 2, 1932. He was drenched in his wife's perfume, lying in front of the full-length mirror in their bedroom, and beside him was the .38 caliber pistol he had used to shoot himself in the head. Instead of calling the police, the butler called the studio, and Louis B. Mayer showed up. The suicide note read:

> Dearest Dear,
> Unfortunately this is the only way to make good the frightful wrong I have done to you, and to wipe out my abject humiliation.
> I love you,
> Paul
> You understand that last night was only a comedy.

Mayer took the note before the police arrived, but turned it in later when the studio publicist insisted he do so. Bern had a secret that was so deep and dark he was ashamed to admit it to the world. He required a phallus to have sexual intercourse with his new wife.

It is rumored that Dorothy Millette, Bern's first wife and a Hollywood starlet in her own right, drowned herself in the Sacramento River after hearing the news the next day.

Another rumor circulated that Millette had contacted Bern soon after his marriage to Harlow asking him to take her back. He told Millette to travel to San Francisco and he would meet her there. There is no evidence confirming this story, but suicide or not, she did drown in the Sacramento River.

Bern's funeral, held at Grace Chapel, was attended by close friends and family. Over 2,000 onlookers gathered outside the church to witness the spectacle. Bern lay in state surrounded by $25,000 worth of flowers, one of the greatest floral tributes seen for a Hollywood memorial to this day. Conrad Nagel delivered the eulogy, stating, "This can't be the end. His gentle spirit is still with us. We bid you Godspeed, Paul Bern, on your journey to a better place and we say here in your own words and in all reverence: 'We'll be seeing you.'"

LOU TELLEGEN

A stage actor who once claimed to be engaged to the great actress Sarah Bernhart (he later retracted the statement), Lou Tellegen felt his suicide should be much more planned out.

Tellegen had been married a grand total of four times during his career. He traveled abroad to play the lead in Oscar Wilde's "The Picture of Dorian Gray," starred in film opposite Dorothy Davenport and Geraldine Farrar, and later married Farrar.

He continued to have great success on the screen until his face was burned in a tragic accident. After this, Tellegen struggled to find work, but continued to live a lavish lifestyle; eventually this led to his filing for bankruptcy.

Then the offer of the lead in the film "Caravan" seemed to be ready to resurrect his career and put Tellegen back in the public eye. Unfortunately, an illness, later determined to be cancer, led to him losing the role. Tellegen became more and more despondent during his six-week stay in the hospital, leading some to speculate that he was experiencing some mental issues as well.

After his release from the hospital, Tellegen stayed at the home of a friend, Mrs. John T. Cuday. She had been a good friend and wanted Tellegen to be comfortable in her home during his recovery. She was unaware of the mental problems and depression plaguing the actor.

On October 29, 1934, Tellegen surrounded himself with the newspaper clippings, photos, and movie posters from his career, took the gold scissors he had used to cut out all of the articles, and stabbed himself to death, Hari-kari style.

He was discovered by Cuday's maid and butler, but he was not dead. The butler ran across the street and summoned Dr. Charles T. Cooper, who assessed the situation and determined there was nothing that could be done for the dying man.

Only thirty-seven people attended the small funeral, a strangely meager turnout for a Hollywood legend who held the adulation of legions of fans just a few years before. Although Tellegen had been married four times, none of his wives attended the memorial.

CHARLES BOYER

Known as the great lover of the silver screen, Charles Boyer was the personification of sophistication and charm. Having a career that spanned more than fifty years, Boyer enjoyed his life in Hollywood and abroad.

Boyer met his only wife, Patricia Paterson, at a dinner party, and they married three months later on February 14, 1934. They had a decades-long marriage (seldom seen in Hollywood) and were extremely happy. Even during the troubled times (their son committed suicide in 1961), they supported each other through it all.

In the late 1970s, Paterson was diagnosed with cancer, and the couple moved to Arizona to seek out a specialist to assist with her treatment. On August 24, 1978, Paterson died quietly with her husband by her side. Boyer was overwrought with grief. Two days later, Boyer had all of the affairs of the family in order, and he took an overdose of Seconal. He was found unconscious, but still alive; rushed to the hospital, Boyer died later that day, which would have been his eighty-first birthday. Husband and wife were buried side by side next to their son.

Charles and Patricia Boyer's headstone can be found at Holy Cross Memorial Park in Culver City, California.

SCOTTY BECKETT

Scotty Beckett began his career at the ripe old age of three with parts in the films, "I Am Suzanne" and "Gallant Lady" in 1933. He was asked to join the cast of the Our Gang series of shorts (later known as The Little Rascals) produced by Hal Roach in 1934, and Beckett's mother heartily accepted. With his large, soulful eyes, oversized sweaters, and side-turned baseball cap, Beckett clearly stood out as sidekick to leader Spanky McFarland.

Unlike his costars, Beckett continued working in major motion pictures in addition to his work with Roach. With the encouragement of his manager and his mother, he left the Our Gang cast in 1935. Beckett was in good company, starring opposite stars like Wallace Beery, Spencer Tracy, Irene Dunne, Charles Boyer, and Cary Grant. Beckett's star continued to climb, and he found steady work during the 1930s and 1940s.

In 1946, he was cast as the young Al Jolson in "The Al Jolson Story," and in 1948, he played opposite Eleanor Powell and Elizabeth Taylor in "A Date with Judy," a light, happy teenage film about kids trying to grow up too fast. Real life would parallel this theme for Beckett. Later that same year, he discovered drugs and alcohol and was arrested for driving while under the influence.

In 1949, he met and began dating tennis star Beverly Baker. They married, but the marriage was over within a few short months. Beckett married a second time, and his son, Scotty Jr., was born from that union.

In 1954, Beckett was arrested for carrying a concealed weapon and attempting to pass a bad check. He continued to have financial difficulties and struggled to find work until he was cast in the television series "Rocky Jones, Space Ranger" in 1955. The show was not popular, and he was released from his contract even before the show was canceled.

Becoming more and more desperate, Beckett continued getting into trouble with the law, drinking, doing drugs, and lashing out in bouts of violence. Eventually, his wife served him with divorce papers.

In 1962, Beckett attempted suicide by slitting his wrists, but failed. He tried and failed to find a new career in real estate. He even tried to go back to school and study medicine for a short time.

On May 10, 1968, Beckett checked himself into a rest home in Hollywood after having been badly beaten. Two days later, he was found dead with a suicide note and bottle of barbiturates by his side. The contents of the suicide note were never released to the public. A small funeral was held in Los Angeles, and Beckett was laid to rest under a simple headstone. He was only thirty-nine years old.

Peg Entwistle

The most famous suicide among the leading ladies of her day was starlet Peg Entwistle. She was a New York actress trying to make it in the glitz and glamour of Hollywood, but instead found herself at the bottom of Mount Lee.

Born Millicent Lilian Entwistle, she began her career on the stage in New York after immigrating to the United States from England with her father and two brothers. Entwistle's father, a stage actor, was brought here by Producer Charles Frohman and performed in comedies until he retired when Entwistle was nine years old. He then was killed while crossing the street, leaving the family destitute. She and her brothers were adopted by their Uncle Charles and Aunt Jane, both of whom retired from the world of the theater to remain close to the children and give them a proper upbringing.

Entwistle found moderate success on the stage and was even credited as the inspiration of great actress Bette Davis. It was reported that Davis had seen Entwistle on the stage in Henrik Ibsen's "The Wild Duck" and told her mother, "I want to be exactly like Peg Entwistle." Later in her career, Davis would confirm this to be true, stating that she felt it was Entwistle's performance that led her to the stage.

Entwistle was originally recruited by the New York Theater Guild and worked with such notables as George M. Cohan and William Gillette. In between Broadway performances, she traveled with the Theater Guild. Entwistle came to Hollywood with the Guild in 1929 for a short run of her current play, but left with the show, choosing to continue her stage acting rather than stay on in Hollywood. She would not see the West Coast again for many years.

It was in May 1932 that Entwistle would travel west to Hollywood to star opposite Billie Burke in the stage production of "The Mad Hope," written by Romney Brent. This West Coast release was designed to see how audiences would like the show prior to the New York debut. The show was a huge success, selling out every performance until it closed on June 4, 1932. Entwistle and her co-stars received rave reviews for their performances.

Entwistle was due to return to New York with the play, but was offered a screen test with RKO Pictures. She agreed to stay and was offered a one-picture deal to costar in "Thirteen Women." Unfortunately, the studio received poor reviews from the critics and negative feedback from audiences during the pre-screening for her performance.

Entwistle was devastated by the news and fell into deep despair. During the years after the Great Depression, money was a rare commodity and Entwistle was broke, unable to return to the New York stage. With no offers to act in films and no stage work to be found, she became increasingly depressed, fearing that her life was at a hopeless end.

On Friday, September 16, 1932, she left the home of her uncle, claiming she was going to visit friends. But instead, she went to the HOLLYWOOD sign at the top of Mount Lee, climbed to the top of the "H" (back then the sign read HOLLYWOODLAND), and jumped into the canyon below. Two days later, following an anonymous tip from a hiker, police found clothing at the base of the "H" and her broken body at the bottom of a ravine. She had left her coat, shoes, and a note at the base of the sign, but she had not signed the note, thereby leaving her identity unknown.

It wasn't until police released the note to the press that her uncle stepped forward, recognizing the initials P.E. at the end of the note. The note read:

> I am afraid I am a coward. I am sorry for everything. If I had done this a long time ago, it would have saved a lot of pain. P.E.

The official cause of death by the Los Angeles coroner was multiple fractures of the pelvis, but experts suspect that Entwistle died of massive trauma and internal bleeding after she jumped, living only a few minutes if at all.

After a small funeral, Entwistle's body was cremated and sent back to Glendale, Ohio, where she was buried next to her father. Her film "Thirteen Women" would not be released until after Entwistle's death. The studio opened the film in New York on

October 15, 1932; some believe it was to capitalize on the news of her sad and tragic death.

It was a tragic ending for a talented actress who was simply trying to make good.

BARBARA LAMARR

One of the most talented women of the early days of Hollywood, Barbara LaMarr was everybody's darling. Most movie stars' accomplishments in Hollywood paled in comparison to those of this most beloved star.

Christened "the girl who is too beautiful," LaMarr began her career when her mother brought her to Hollywood at the age of thirteen. Born Reatha Dale Watson, she began performing under her given name, dancing in Los Angeles theaters. Because LaMarr was a voluptuous young girl, her mother hoped to pass her off as much older. She was arrested for dancing in a house of Burlesque and a judge remanded her to her parents' care; she was only fourteen.

While auditioning for one director, it was rumored that she slapped his face after he tried to kiss and touch her, thereby ending her chance to start her career with that director.

When LaMarr was sixteen, she moved to Yuma, Arizona, where she met and married her first husband, Jack Lytell. Within a few months, the young girl was a widow; her husband died suddenly of a bout with pneumonia after riding the range during a thunderstorm.

Still hoping to make it big, she moved back to Hollywood and changed her name to Barbara LaMarr. Soon after her arrival back in Tinseltown, she met and married handsome attorney Lawrence Converse. Unfortunately for young LaMarr, her new husband neglected to inform her that he was already married and had three children. He was arrested and charged with bigamy. Witnesses said Converse was so devastated at the thought of being separated from LaMarr that he beat his head repeatedly on the bars of his cell, causing four blood clots to form on his brain. He died three days later of complications during surgery.

LaMarr married her third husband, Phil Ainsworth, in 1916, but they divorced a year later when she discovered he had been forging checks to pay for lavish jewels, clothing, and trips. He was tried and convicted of his crimes and sent to San Quentin prison, leaving LaMarr behind.

Barbara LaMarr crypt at Hollywood Forever cemetery in Hollywood, California.

LaMarr resumed dancing, this time with partner Rudolph Valentino at a local club, Harlowe's, in Los Angeles. It was during this time that she met writer Ernest Hemmingway. The two had a brief but torrid love affair, and rumor has it this was neither her first nor only affair during this time. She continued dancing with her new partner, Ben Deely, whom she married a year later, in 1918.

During this time, LaMarr began writing and had several successful screenplays picked up by United Artists Pictures. In 1920, she began acting in bit parts and caught the eye of swashbuckler Douglas Fairbanks, who cast LaMarr as a smoldering vampire in his film "The Nut." He tapped her talents again in the epic film "The Three Musketeers" in 1921. She won that role, coming out ahead of hundreds of other hopefuls.

By this time, LaMarr was contracted with Metro. She suffered an injury on the set of "Souls for Sale" and was administered morphine for the pain so that she could continue working full-time. Little did she know that this seemly benign incident would lead her down a very dark path. Drugs and alcohol would soon play a major part in her life.

By 1923, LaMarr and her fourth husband had separated. Their divorce was not yet final when she married Jack Daughtry, a western movie actor. Ben Deely came back into LaMarr's life to sue her before a Los Angeles judge. The divorce would soon be final, but not before she and Daughtry separated.

LaMarr was becoming one of the top movie stars in Hollywood, with successes like the epic film "The Prisoner of Zenda" in 1922 and "Thy Name is Woman" in 1924. Her peers and the critics considered her the greatest actress of her time. She received rave reviews for all her films, but the raven-haired beauty's lifestyle would soon catch up with her.

LaMarr claimed that she needed no more than two hours of sleep a day because "life was too short to waste any of it by sleeping." LaMarr believed in excess in everything, so she ate, drank, and pushed her body to extremes. By 1924, she could no longer cope with the excessive partying, eating, drinking, and morphine addiction that had plagued her for years. When the effects began to show, she would put herself on a diet of just cocaine and liquids to shed the pounds. This behavior started her health on a downward spiral from which she never did recover. Toward the end of 1925, she suffered a mental breakdown and contracted tuberculosis as a result of the strain of the drugs on her body. This eventually led her to isolate herself in her Alta Dena home, which had been purchased for her by ardent admirer Paul Bern, who had been begging LaMarr for years to marry him. He even attempted suicide when she married Daughtry.

While Hollywood still considers Barbara LaMarr to be one of the greatest beauties to ever grace the silver screen, she had few friends in the last years of her life. Paul Bern was one of these. He remained a loyal friend and cared for her until her death on January 30, 1926. When LaMarr died, the official cause of death was listed as anorexia. Those who knew her well whispered that she had died of a drug overdose or complications from tuberculosis. She was only twenty-nine years old.

The funeral that followed was staged as carefully as any major motion picture LaMarr had starred in during her life. She lay in an open casket laden with flowers while 40,000 fans and admirers filed past her coffin. She was laid to rest in the Cathedral Mausoleum in Hollywood Memorial Park (now called Hollywood Forever Cemetery). Her epitaph reads: "With God in the Joy and Beauty of Youth."

LUPE VELEZ

Dark-haired, dark-eyed beauty Lupe Velez was born in Mexico. At the age of thirteen, Velez was put in a convent school because her family considered her too rambunctious for a little girl. This did little to quell her enthusiasm for life.

As she grew older, Velez helped her family financially by becoming a salesgirl, giving almost all of her money to them, keeping aside only a little for her dancing lessons. In 1924, Velez began performing on the stage. Audiences loved her natural dancing ability, fiery personality, and voluptuous figure. By 1927, Velez was ready to move to the United States and conquer Hollywood.

She began dancing in a musical revue along with future star Fanny Brice. She was discovered by Douglas Fairbanks, who cast her for a role in "The Gaucho."

Velez had many affairs, including several with some of the most notable men of the era — from John Gilbert to Gary Cooper and Johnny Weissmuller, whom she eventually married in 1933. The marriage to Weissmuller was short-lived; they divorced in 1938. Several people claimed their "love" was more "love/hate," particularly when Velez left scratches and red marks on Weissmuller's chest that had to be covered up with makeup during the filming of "Tarzan." After the divorce, she was cast with Leon Errol in the "Mexican Spitfire" television series, a testament to Velez's famous temper and infectious humor. The series lasted until 1943.

Velez's career began to fade. She began having affairs more frequently, but the men were becoming less notable. Her partners slid slowly from stars to featured players to stuntmen and ended with the sleazy hangers-on of Hollywood.

Around this time, Velez discovered she was pregnant by Harald Maresch, her latest fling. Being a devout Roman Catholic, she couldn't bear the thought of an abortion, so she decided on a "better" solution. Velez chose to bring the drama of the silver screen into her real life by staging her own elaborate suicide. She lived in a palatial estate, but the mortgage was very overdue, the debts were mounting, and she didn't have a dime to her name.

In this golden era of Hollywood, the elite lived with the belief that the world owed them something just by virtue of their status in Hollywood. Thus, Velez ordered a sumptuous banquet from the local market and deli on credit. She then ordered flowers that would make any bride on her wedding day green with envy. Velez set the stage for this night like a director of a multi-million dollar epic film.

That night, she invited her two best friends (Estelle Taylor and Benita Oakie) to her home for dinner. Once the feast was over, they began talking over brandy and cigarettes. Velez said to her friends, "I am tired of life. I have to fight for everything. I am so tired of it all. Ever since I was a baby in Mexico, I've been fighting. It's my baby. I can't commit murder and still live with myself. I would rather kill myself."

At 3 o'clock in the morning, Velez climbed the stairs to her bedroom in her silver gown. She had laid out the room like a shrine before the party, with flowers and candles everywhere. She wrote a quick note and left it on the nightstand.

> To Harald,
>   May God forgive you and forgive me too, but I prefer to take my life away and our baby's before I bring him with shame or killing him.
>   Lupe

On the back of the note, she added a postscript:

> How could you, Harald, fake such a great love for me and our baby when all the time you didn't want us? I see no other way out for me so goodbye and good luck to you.
>   Love,
>   Lupe

She had purchased a bottle of Seconal earlier that day and now took all seventy-five tablets with a glass of water. Then she lay on the satin coverlet below a large crucifix, with her hands folded on her breast and eyes closed, picturing in her mind the headlines and photos the next day. Unfortunately for Velez, the headlines would not be anything close to what she had in mind. The actuality would be a much juicier story than she could have dreamed.

When the maid entered Velez's bedroom the next morning, Velez was not on the bed or even in the room. The only evidence of where she might be was a trail of vomit on the rug, heading toward the bathroom. It was there that the maid found the once-great Lupe Velez on the floor of the adjoining bathroom, dead from what appeared to be a hit on the head.

Apparently, the Seconal, mixed with the alcohol and rich food, began to come back up, waking Velez from her slumber. She became violently sick and tried to make her way to the bathroom. According to legends passed down through the years, Lupe hit her head on the toilet either in an attempt to reach the bowl or she fainted and hit her head in the fall. There is no substantial proof to the claims that she was found with her head actually in the toilet, the victim of an accidental drowning. I'm sure if she had known in advance the humiliation that would follow her into death, she would have thought twice about the whole affair.

The funeral in Mexico for Lupe Velez was attended by over 4,000 fans and admirers. Several people were injured in the rush for one last look at the fallen star. Velez's sister Reyna fainted and was trampled by the throng. At the cemetery, several headstones were knocked over in the rush to watch the star being laid to rest in the ground.

ONA MUNSON

Ona Munson is best known for the saucy role of madam Belle Watlin in the film classic "Gone with the Wind." Munson began her career on the stage at age sixteen with parts in "No No Nanette" and "Twinkle Twinkle," opposite fellow film great Joe E. Brown. She continued her success on the stage with the 1927 hit "Hold Everything" and "You're the Cream in My Coffee" became her signature song throughout her Vaudeville years.

It wasn't until Munson auditioned for director David O. Selznick and landed the role of Madam Belle Watlin that she would create film history in the classic "Gone with the Wind." Rumors were whispered all across the country that the great Mae West would be playing the role, but this proved to be a Hollywood publicity stunt to generate interest in the movie.

After the acclaim of "Gone with the Wind," Munson repeatedly found herself cast in the role of saloon girls and, in 1941, played Madam Mother Gin Sling in "The Shanghai Gesture." Afterward, she would be credited in only six films, and those were just bit parts. Her last role was playing opposite Edward G. Robinson in "The Red House" in 1949.

With her career all but over, Munson struggled to accept obscurity. It wasn't until the 1950s, when her health began to decline, that she took her own life by overdosing on barbiturates. Munson was found dead in the New York apartment she shared with her third husband, Eugene Berman. She was fifty-one. The note left behind was simple and brief:

> This is the only way I know to be free again. Please don't follow me.

Ona Munson left a lasting legacy in her most cherished role, that of the kind-hearted confidante to the dashing Rhett Butler.

Side Note: Ona wasn't the only actor from "Gone With the Wind" to die tragically, nor was she the only one to receive accolades for her performance in the epic movie. "Gone With the Wind" earned ten Academy Awards in 1940 and ranks number four among the American Film Institute's 100 Top American Films of All Time.

DOROTHY DANDRIDGE

Considered one of the most beautiful women of her time, Dorothy Dandridge suffered a life and career fraught with struggle. She was born into a show business family — her mother and grandmother had both performed on the stage — and began her career as a child, performing with her sisters. Dandridge's mother had trained her daughters in singing, dancing, music, and recitation.

With the advent of the Great Depression in 1929, Dandridge's mother moved her family to Hollywood. Combining forces with Etta Jones, the girls aptly named "The Dandridge Sisters" began singing in Los Angeles nightclubs. The sisters then got a bigger opportunity, being offered film roles in "The Big Broadcast" of 1939 and "A Day at the Races," starring the Marx Brothers.

In 1941, Dandridge broke off from her sisters and filmed "Sunset Valley Serenade" with Harold Nicholas of the Nicholas Brothers fame. They were married in 1942, and Dorothy became pregnant

Dorothy Dandridge Niche at Forest Lawn Memorial Park in Glendale, California.

with their first child that same year. Her world was shattered when she gave birth and discovered that her newborn daughter had a brain disorder. Adding to her troubles, her husband was known for his many affairs during the marriage. The stress and infidelity led her to divorce Nicholas in 1949.

Dandridge focused all of her energies on her career, taking acting and dancing lessons. She created a new nightclub act for herself and toured the United States and Europe. In 1954, she auditioned for the lead in Otto Preminger's "Carmen Jones." He turned her down for the part, but Dandridge disguised herself and went for a second audition. He cast her immediately, and shortly thereafter, the two were involved romantically, even though Preminger was married. She was nominated for an Academy Award for her work in the film, the first time ever that an African-American woman was nominated for an Oscar. She also graced the cover of *Life* magazine, another first.

Even with her achievements in film, Dandridge continued to struggle for parts. The parts she did receive, however, garnered her much critical acclaim for her acting and singing ability.

In 1959, Dandridge met restaurateur Jack Denison and, within a few months, they were married. Denison squandered all of the money Dandridge had brought into the marriage and any that she earned during, leaving her bankrupt. She was forced to put her daughter in a state-run institution since she could no longer afford private nursing care. She began drinking heavily and taking drugs to help with the emotional pain of her life. In 1965, Dandridge made the decision to get clean and checked herself into a health spa to rid herself of her addictions.

She was scheduled to perform at Manhattan's Basin Street East and readied herself for the journey. She was also being offered two film roles that required her to travel to Mexico for shooting before she went to New York. The day before she boarded the plane for Mexico, she twisted her ankle and X-rays confirmed she had fractures, causing severe pain. She continued working in Mexico and planned to seek medical attention upon her return to Los Angeles.

Dandridge returned to Los Angeles and began packing for her trip east. She spoke with her mother on the phone that evening, informing her that her manager, Earl Mills, was scheduled to pick her up the next morning at 7:15 to have her foot set in a cast. Later that night, Dandridge called Mills, asking to postpone the appointment. "I'll sleep for a while, and I'll be fine," she said and hung up the phone.

When Mills arrived at Dandridge's apartment the following morning, he knocked on her door, but there was no answer. He continued to pound on the door, finally breaking into the apartment. He found Dandridge lying on the floor wearing nothing but a scarf wrapped around her head. The coroner concluded she had been dead for two hours when Mills found her body. A preliminary coroner's report stated that she had died of an embolism caused by the fracture to her ankle. A later, more thorough report revealed that she had overdosed on Tofranil, an antidepressant the doctor had prescribed. Questions arose as to whether or not this was an accidental overdose when a note was found in the apartment:

> In case of my death, don't remove anything I have on: scarf, gown, or underwear. Cremate me right away. If I have anything—money, furniture—get it to my mother Ruby Dandridge. She will know what to do.
>
> Dorothy

A memorial service was held in the Little Church of the Flowers at Forest Lawn Memorial Park in Glendale, California. Dandridge was cremated per her wishes. She had a total of two dollars and some change in the bank at the time of her death at the age of forty-two.

Carole Landis

Another of the Hollywood starlets desperate to find fame and love in the glamour of Tinseltown was Carole Landis.

Given the name Frances Ridste at birth, Landis was born to a middle-class family. When she was still a young child, her father abandoned the family, and her mother moved them out west. Landis continued her education, but met a young man named Irving Wheeler at school. The love-struck teenagers eloped to Yuma, Arizona. Since Landis was only fifteen years old at the time, the marriage was annulled within a few weeks. The two continued to stay committed to each other and were remarried in 1934 when she was of age. Again, the marriage was not destined to last. By 1935, the two had separated, and Landis took a bus to San Francisco. That was when she changed her name from Frances Ridste to Carole Landis and began working at the Royal Hawaiian Club as a hula dancer. Then she took a job as a lead singer with the Carl Ravazza Orchestra.

With some success behind her, Landis decided it was time for her to conquer Hollywood and moved to Los Angeles. Immediately, both Landis's mother and Landis's estranged husband joined her, hoping to cash in on any success she might have.

In 1937, Landis was hired as an extra in "A Star Is Born" and "A Day at the Races." Soon after, she was given a small feature role in "Variety Show." It was thanks to this role that Landis was offered a fifty-dollar-a-week contract with Warner Brothers. Unfortunately, she received only minor roles during this time. Due to the lack of press on the starlet, the studio let her contract lapse in 1938.

Landis received no help from her family either. Her husband is reported to have sued Producer/Director Busby Berkeley in court, claiming that Berkeley had caused his wife to alienate him and stolen her affections. A Los Angeles judge dismissed the case, but the damage to Landis's career could not easily be undone.

Throughout 1938 and 1939, Landis continued to struggle in her career; she was playing only minor roles and receiving one liner's in few pictures.

In 1940, Landis received her next big break. Hal Roach was working on a new picture, "One Million B.C.," and offered her the lead role. She happily accepted and decided to give herself a new look for the part. After having plastic surgery on her nose and dying her hair platinum blonde, Landis felt ready to tackle her new screen role. Roach approved of the new look and launched a publicity campaign dubbing her as "The Best Legs in Town" and "The Ping Girl" (supposedly short for purring), a moniker she hated. The movie was a huge success, and Landis felt she was finally destined for greatness.

Landis divorced her husband and found a new romance with yacht broker Willis Hunt, Jr. They were married in July 1940, but by November of that same year, the romance had turned sour and the two were quickly divorced. After the divorce was final, Landis stated, "We should have just remained friends."

Landis continued working steadily, but Darryl Zanuck took a personal interest in her and purchased her contract from Hal Roach. She attracted much studio attention, and he seemed to be quite infatuated with her. As is often the case with studio executives, his fondness waned, and Landis found she was being cast in smaller pictures with less screen time.

When Landis was offered a chance to go on a tour of Ireland and England with some of her fellow actresses, she quickly accepted the job. Soon after arriving in Europe, she met naval aviator Thomas Wallace and impulsively married within a few weeks of meeting.

On her next USO tour, Landis became gravely ill, contracting malaria and dysentery. By the next fall, she and her new husband had also fallen apart and went to Reno for another quickie divorce.

In 1945, Landis appeared on Broadway and, after a brief courtship, married her producer, W. Horace Schmidlapp. Although she found modest success on the stage, she was still under contract with 20th Century Fox and thus destined to return, eventually, to Hollywood. When she did return to Hollywood, she made two more forgettable pictures.

Landis met actor Rex Harrison in 1947, and the two began a steamy affair. Although she was still married to Schmidlapp at the time, Landis carried on the affair out in the open. Harrison, though, was married too, and he wanted to keep things quiet. Landis transferred to the London studio to be closer to Harrison and began divorce proceedings to end her marriage to Schmidlapp.

By 1948, Landis's divorce was final, and she returned to Hollywood with Harrison in tow. The two continued seeing each other while Landis worked on her latest picture, "Unfaithfully Yours." Publicly, Harrison continued to deny the rumors of their affair, stating to the press, "We are great friends, and that is all."

On July 4, 1948, Landis invited Harrison to her house for a quiet dinner. She told him about her concerns financially, but he tired quickly of this conversation and left around 9 o'clock that evening. Landis became very distraught and made several telephone calls, looking for a friendly voice to talk to. Unfortunately for her, this would prove difficult, since it was a holiday weekend and everyone was away. Later in the evening, Landis started drinking heavily and in her stupor made up her mind to end the affair once and for all.

She took out a small suitcase and packed all of the love letters she had received from Harrison during their time together. She drove to the home of Roland Culvers and his wife, where Harrison was staying. She left the suitcase on the doorstep. Landis wanted to make sure Harrison received the suitcase, but she also wanted to drop it off anonymously.

After the errand was complete, Landis returned to her home. Once there, she went into the master bathroom, where she pulled a bottle of Seconal from the cabinet. Landis took the entire bottle and lay down on the bathroom floor with her head resting on her jewel case.

The next day, Harrison called the house, but Landis's maid informed him that she had not seen Landis and that Landis was not responding to knocks on the locked bedroom door. Harrison drove to the house that afternoon, gravely concerned for Landis by this time.

Harrison forced his way into the bathroom and found Landis lying on her side, dead at the age of twenty-nine. An autopsy revealed high amounts of alcohol and Seconal in her blood. It was also determined that she had attempted to stand up just prior to her death. Had she changed her mind and tried to get help? We will never know.

After the police investigation was completed, Harrison left the house and returned to the Culvers' home. Upon his arrival, his friends pointed out the suitcase that had been left on the doorstep. Harrison opened it, revealing the many letters he had sent to Landis during their courtship.

The funeral for Carole Landis was attended by many of Hollywood's brightest stars of the era. Pall-bearers Cesar Romero, Dick Haymes, and Pat O'Brien carried the casket containing the young starlet to its final resting place. Landis was dressed in a dazzling evening gown with an orchid pinned to each shimmering strap. Around her neck was the gold cross that her friend Diana Lewis had given her. She had been so touched by the gift that she wore it every day.

Harrison spoke out publicly about the death, stating he had no guilt, but it was later discovered that he had spent many months under a psychiatrist's care after her death. His contract was torn up, and he was branded a villain in Hollywood for many years after the tragic event.

Years before her death, Landis spoke on the suicide of actress Lupe Velez, "I know how Lupe Velez felt. You fight just so long, and then you begin to worry about being washed up. You fear there's only one way to go, and that's down."

Chapter Two:

UNSOLVED MYSTERIES

Some of the greatest stories to come from Hollywood had nothing to do with the scripts that were made into our favorite movies. Throughout the history of Tinseltown, the mysterious deaths surrounding great movie stars have been the proof of the old adage about truth being stranger than fiction. Many of these tales have been told and retold throughout the years. From the earliest film stars to today's A-list superstars, the world clamors most for those stories with an aura of mystery or even outright foul play, especially if there are no clues as to what really happened or who did it.

VIRGINIA RAPPE

Who, you may ask, is Virginia Rappe? While she is not one of our more famous or acclaimed actresses in the history of Hollywood, the life and death of Virginia Rappe is one of the most legendary of the twentieth century.

Very little is known about Rappe's life at the turn-of-the-century, but those who knew her claimed she was born in New York around 1895. Born to a mother who danced for a living, she grew up very poor. Her mother died when she was eleven, and young Rappe became an orphan. She was sent to live with relatives in Chicago, and it was there that she began modeling at the local department store when she was just sixteen years old. It is rumored that during this time Rappe gave birth to a child, but there are no records to substantiate this. However, records were not kept as often or as accurately as they are today, so it is possible that she did in fact have a child.

Grave of Virginia Rappe at Hollywood Forever Cemetery in Hollywood, California

Soon, modeling was not enough for the pretty young girl. She set her sights on the dream factory of Hollywood. Packing up her few possessions, Rappe made the trip out west and soon found herself working occasionally as an extra at Keystone Studios, home to great actors like Buster Keaton, Mabel Normand, Charlie Chaplin, and Roscoe "Fatty" Arbuckle.

In 1917, Rappe began working for Fred Balshofer. She had a prominent role in the film "Paradise Garden" opposite the very popular actor Harold Lockwood. Once again, rumors spread that Rappe gave birth to another child in 1918 and that it was given up to foster care to avoid complications to her career. Also in 1918, Rappe starred opposite early film star Rudolph Valentino in the film "Over the Rhine." It was for her efforts in that film that she won the title of "best-dressed girl in pictures."

During this time, Rappe became involved with director Henry "Pathe" Lehrman and soon the two were engaged. He cast Rappe in at least four known films. There may have been more than this, but none of the original film has survived. Continuing her burgeoning success, Rappe became the face girl for the popular tune "Let Me Call You Sweetheart."

Through her relationship with Lehrman, Rappe met Roscoe "Fatty" Arbuckle, who offered her a role in his next film. This was a high point in the career of funnyman Fatty Arbuckle; he had just signed a $3 million-dollar contract with the studio. Arbuckle decided this needed to be celebrated and invited all of his Hollywood friends to accompany him to San Francisco for Labor Day weekend. Rappe had another commitment that would not allow her to leave town with the others, but she flew to San Francisco and met up with the group that weekend.

During the festivities over the three days, Arbuckle was accused of raping Rappe. Maude Delmont, Rappe's friend, made the allegations against Arbuckle, but they were never proven. The actress died at Pine Street Hospital on September 10, 1921 of peritonitis caused by a ruptured bladder, but the rumors of the events of that weekend painted Arbuckle as a maniac who had killed Rappe.

It didn't take long for the San Francisco police to arrest Fatty Arbuckle for the rape and murder of Virginia Rappe. The newspapers received word of the girl's death, and even before an investigation could begin, the headlines read: "ARBUCKLE ORGY RAPER DANCES WHILE VICTIM DIES." Irresponsible journalism ran away with the story, each tabloid attempting to make more outrageous claims than the next. One even asserted that Rappe had died of a "hideously unnatural rape." They claimed that Arbuckle flew into a rage at Rappe after he could not perform due to his inebriation and raped the poor girl with a champagne bottle. One newspaper claimed that Arbuckle's 266-pound frame actually crushed the girl when he took a flying leap across the room and landed on top of her.

Although Arbuckle hadn't been convicted of the crime, church and religious groups demanded that his films be banned, and one group in Connecticut actually tore down the movie screen during a screening of a Fatty Arbuckle film.

Fatty Arbuckle went to trial in November 1921 for the murder of film starlet Virginia Rappe. Arbuckle's attorney was able to get the charge reduced from first-degree murder to manslaughter. Arbuckle claimed no wrongdoing and denied all of the charges. His lawyers painted Rappe as a girl with loose morals and a habit of sleeping around.

In his sworn testimony, Arbuckle stated that on September 5, 1921, he found Rappe lying on the floor of his bathroom in agony and attempted to assist the girl by placing ice on her abdomen. He then put her to bed, where in her pain she tore at her clothing. Arbuckle claimed he asked his fellow partygoers to place her into a cold bath and then summoned a doctor when the cold bath did not help her either. The doctor diagnosed Rappe as being drunk and gave her morphine for whatever pain she was experiencing. It was after the group of partiers left the hotel and returned to Los Angeles that Rappe was sent to the hospital and later died.

Virginia Rappe's body was returned to Hollywood. Her fiancé Lehrman made little fuss over the funeral arrangements; he sent a blanket of lilies for her casket. Though it was only a few months after Rappe's burial that Lehrman went on to marry another young starlet (Jocelyn Lee), after his death he was buried by Rappe's side, where he remains to this day.

Eventually, Arbuckle was brought to trial. After three trials and two hung juries, he was finally acquitted. At the final trial, in addition to being acquitted, Arbuckle received a written apology from the jury. The apology is supposed to have read:

Acquittal is not enough for Roscoe Arbuckle. We feel that a great injustice has been done him… There was not the slightest proof adduced to connect him in any way with the commission of a crime. He was manly throughout the case and told a straightforward story which we all believed… We wish him success and hope that the American people will take the judgment of fourteen men and women that Roscoe Arbuckle is entirely innocent and free from all blame.

It was after the final trial that witness Maude Delmont would be accused of issuing false testimony. Although the note was never found, a rumor circulated that Delmont sent a note to one of her contemporaries stating, "Got Arbuckle right where I want him. Big payoff coming."

Later, another story would emerge stating that Rappe was in fact pregnant at the time of the scandal and that the hospital had removed her internal female organs to cover up the pregnancy.

In either case, the promising career of a lovely young girl with dreams of stardom ended that fateful day, and the career of jolly, funny Roscoe "Fatty" Arbuckle would never again be what it once was. An unforgiving audience would no longer see his films. He was forced to work behind the scenes under an assumed name until he was finally offered a return to the screen in June 1933.

Arbuckle and his wife celebrated their first anniversary and his return to film by going out to dinner. Afterward, they returned to their apartment and retired for the evening. After midnight, Arbuckle's wife checked on her husband and attempted to speak to him. She received no answer. He had passed away sometime after going to bed. The cause of death would later be determined to be a heart attack. He was forty-six years old.

After the police concluded their investigation, Arbuckle's body was transported to the Frank E. Campbell Funeral Home, where he was dressed in a dark grey suit, white shirt, and the ever-present bow tie. His grey steel casket with silver handles was set up for visitation in the famous Gold Room, the same chamber that had held the body of Rudolph Valentino years before.

Over 12,000 fans and admirers soberly passed the casket for one last look at the great comedian who fell from grace. An estimated 1,000 children also attended. Respected stars of the day Charlie Chaplin and Buster Keaton were among those who sent flowers. Celebrated actors Bert Lahr and Ray McCarey were in attendance, and Will Rogers gave a touching eulogy.

After the memorial, Arbuckle's wife had his body cremated, per his wishes. The remains were returned to her, and she honored him one last time by having Arbuckle scattered in the Pacific Ocean.

WILLIAM DESMOND TAYLOR

Another of our unsolved, mysterious Hollywood deaths concerned the great William Desmond Taylor, who came to Hollywood in 1912 as an actor and began directing in 1914. Soon Taylor would be director for the biggest studios in Hollywood, becoming quite a ladies' man and public figure in Hollywood.

On the cold, quiet night of February 1, 1922, Taylor had spent the evening in the company of one of the biggest actresses in Hollywood, Mabel Normand. They had been drinking bootleg gin, discussing movies, and playing the piano in the study of his apartment on Alvarado Street. Shortly after 7:30 p.m., Taylor walked Normand to her car, and the driver took her home. She would be the last person to see William Desmond Taylor alive.

Around 8 p.m., Taylor's neighbors heard what sounded like a car backfiring on the street. Two of them, Faith Maclean and

The crypt of William Desmond Taylor bears his legal name at the Cathedral Mausoleum.

Hazel Gillon, stated that they both looked out their windows just in time to see a dark figure in an overcoat, scarf, and hat walking quickly down the sidewalk. Later, MacLean told police that the figure had a strange walk, almost effeminate. She honestly could not testify whether the person was a man or a woman.

It would not be until the next morning that Taylor's manservant, Henry Peavey, would find Taylor's body lying on the floor. Neighbor Edna Purivance called Mabel Normand, who, in turn, called Charles Eyton, the manger of the famous Lasky Players. It was Eyton who contacted Adolph Zukor, the head of Paramount Studios. Neighbor Purivance also felt compelled to call movie star Mary Miles Minter, who was another of Taylor's many lady friends. Minter was unavailable, and a message was left with her mother, Charlotte Shelby, who had also allegedly had an affair with Taylor. It is interesting to note that of all the people notified of the death, *not* one person called the Los Angeles Police Department. Each person had business to attend to at Taylor's home prior to the police being allowed entry.

Normand was the first to arrive on the scene. She busied herself searching for letters and other correspondence. Eyton was busy getting rid of the illegal liquor on the premises. Zukor had already lost one of his biggest box office stars because of the Arbuckle scandal earlier that year and was on the scene to remove any illicit pornography and evidence of Taylor's many affairs, both of which might damage his name. Shelby, with her daughter Minter in tow, arrived at the Taylor bungalow to retrieve her property.

There lay William Desmond Taylor's body on the floor, sprawled out with arms stretched wide and legs pinned down by a chair. Meanwhile, no one paid the body any mind. The police later surmised that significant clues were destroyed in the fireplace long before they arrived on the scene.

Fortunately for the police, they arrived before the house was completely stripped of all the evidence. They found a large cache of pornographic photographs hidden in a drawer. The photos were of Taylor with several of the day's top starlets.

Normand was questioned about her contribution to the cleanup of the apartment. She stated candidly that she had been searching for letters she had written to Taylor. She wanted to prevent them from falling into the wrong hands and being misconstrued by outsiders. Later, some of the letters in question were found in one of Taylor's riding boots; others were found between the pages of a book in the study. These letters were on pink monogrammed stationery with the initials M.M.M. Twenty-year-old Mary Miles Minter, one of Paramount's biggest stars, had written letters to the much older Taylor stating, for example:

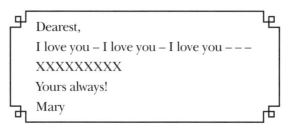

Dearest,

I love you – I love you – I love you – – –

XXXXXXXXX

Yours always!

Mary

Once the evidence of her affection was found, Minter admitted that she loved him deeply and tenderly, with all the admiration a young girl gives to a man with the poise and position of Taylor.

Even with all of the commotion at the house, no arrests were made. The funeral that followed was something right out of the Hollywood sound stages.

An open casket draped with the British flag lay in the crowded memorial service. The aisle displayed a table and chair used by Desmond at his studio office covered with a display of violets. Flowers sent by Hollywood elite Wallace Reid, Charlie Chaplin, Agnes Ayers, Betty Compton, and Douglas MacLean created a backdrop behind the casket.

Devoted manservant Henry Peavey became hysterical during the service and was escorted out of the church until the casket was removed at the conclusion of the memorial.

Mabel Normand arrived and, with the assistance of police, was allowed passage through the enormous crowd trying to push their way into the church. Visibly distraught, Normand fainted at the conclusion of the service and stayed in the chapel until the throngs of people could be dispersed outside.

It is rumored that a devastated Mary Miles Minter walked up to the casket and kissed the corpse full on the lips. Upon breaking the kiss, Minter announced that Taylor had spoken to her from beyond the grave, whispering, "I shall love you always, Mary!"

Pallbearers Frank Beal, William Young, Frank Lloyd, William De Mille, George Melford, Arthur Hoyt, and Charles Eyton carried the casket to the waiting hearse. After the funeral circus was over, William Desmond Taylor was interred in the Cathedral Mausoleum at Hollywood Memorial Park (now known as Hollywood Forever Cemetery).

But the story doesn't end there.

While the life and tragic death of Taylor was like something out of a movie script, the Hollywood elite with whom he spent his days and nights would have been stunned to learn about the life Taylor left behind before coming to Hollywood.

Born in Ireland and named William Cunningham Deane-Tanner, Taylor lived with his family until the age of eighteen, when he had a falling out with his father. He immigrated to the United States and found work as an engineer, an actor, and even a gold miner in Alaska for a short period.

Taylor met and married Ethel May Harrison, and they had a daughter together while he worked in her father's antique shop in New York. On a quiet day in 1908, Taylor went to lunch and never returned to his work or family. When co-workers were questioned as to his whereabouts, no one knew. He had disappeared without a word to anyone. While his family was left devastated in New York, Taylor moved on with his life, changed his name, and lived in anonymity until his appearance as a Hollywood actor in 1912.

Another twist to this odd tale involves Taylor's brother Denis Deane-Tanner. Denis apparently followed his brother's lead. He also left his family, went to California, and worked for his sibling as a butler. On the night of the murder, Denis Deane-Tanner vanished and never returned to the Alvarado Street bungalow. Was Taylor really carrying on an affair with Mary Miles Minter and her mother, Charlotte Shelby? Could jealousy have been the catalyst for such a heinous crime of passion? Perhaps the wife Taylor had left behind so many years ago could have been the murderer? He had reconciled with his estranged daughter many years after his disappearance, so it's not difficult to believe that Ethel May Harrison could have discovered Taylor's whereabouts. Or could the murderer have been the great comedic actress Mabel Normand? Normand, a notorious cocaine user, had found out that Taylor was heading the move to drive the drug dealers out of Hollywood. Could that have been enough to motivate her to kill?

While speculation continues, with the cast of characters reading like the credits to an epic Hollywood drama, we will probably never really know who killed the man known to Hollywood as William Desmond Taylor.

Side Note: While visiting the Cathedral Mausoleum where Taylor was laid to rest, I noticed that the crypt plate bears his given name, William Deane-Tanner.

Tom Ince

Tom who, you ask? While Tom Ince may not be one of the better-known personalities of the Hollywood elite, his life and death take center stage as one of the twentieth century's great Hollywood scandals.

Ince began his career on the stage in New York, traveling in Vaudeville shows. He began working as an actor in very early films, but the work was sporadic, and he needed something with a more reliable income. That was how he came to be a promoter and then a lifeguard while continuing to act part-time. It wasn't long before Ince began directing and producing his own films, which led to the inevitable move west to the lights of Hollywood.

Once he arrived, he went to work for Universal Pictures and built his own western town in Santa Monica dubbed "Inceville." Ince was known as the father of cowboy westerns and with good reason. He made over 150 films in 1913 alone! Together with partners D. W. Griffith and Mack Sennett, Ince formed Triangle Pictures. Later, he joined forces with rival Adolph Zukor to create Paramount Pictures.

In 1924, Ince was approached by millionaire newspaper man William Randolph Hearst, who wanted make the Paramount lot the new home for his production company Cosmopolitan Productions. The two were in negotiations when Hearst and his mistress, Marion Davies, invited Ince and his mistress, actress Margaret Livingston, and thirteen other "A-list" celebrities out on their yacht for a weekend in San Diego. This also turned into a celebration of Ince's forty-third birthday.

Though Ince accepted the invitation, he was unable to board the yacht in San Pedro with contemporaries Charlie Chaplin, Aileen Pringle, and Hollywood newcomer Louella Parsons. The premier of his latest picture, "The Mirage," kept him in Los Angeles, but he agreed to meet the party in San Diego later that evening. The group boarded Hearst's yacht, named *The Oneida*, along with a full jazz band and enough bottles of liquor to sustain the group for the weekend.

Over the course of the weekend, Ince fell ill and had to be taken ashore to the local hospital. He was escorted by Hearst's private physician. He later died; the cause of death was recorded as acute indigestion. Almost immediately, a rumor began making the rounds that Ince had in fact been shot while aboard the yacht by none other than Hearst himself.

Whatever the real story was, the guests onboard *The Oneida* were not talking. The next morning, the *Los Angeles Times* ran the headline:

"MOVIE PRODUCER SHOT ON HEARST YACHT"

Not surprisingly, by that evening, the headline had changed, and no other paper ran a story.

The funeral service was held in private with only the family, Marion Davies, Charlie Chaplin, Mary Pickford, Douglas Fairbanks, and Harold Lloyd attending. The body was cremated immediately after the service. Ince's wife moved back to Europe and never returned to the United States.

The only person to come forward after Ince's death was Dr. Daniel Carson Goodman, Hearst's personal physician, who had been on the boat that evening. Rumors had been spreading quickly through staff members who had been onboard that night, claiming someone had seen Ince leaving the boat with a gunshot wound. The doctor recounted the events very differently.

According to Goodman, Ince had arrived on the yacht early Sunday morning. He seemed fine, but did complain of being tired after the long day before. He ate some dinner and retired to his cabin along with the other guests that evening. He awoke early the next morning before the other guests had begun to stir. He complained of having difficulty sleeping during the night due to a bout of indigestion and was still feeling ill. At the next stop, Goodman and Ince exited the yacht, and Ince complained of chest pains near his heart. The two men boarded a train, but got off in Del Mar, just north of San Diego, when the pain in Ince's chest worsened. They checked into a hotel and Ince lay down in bed to rest. Meanwhile, Goodman contacted Ince's wife to notify her of her husband's condition. He also contacted another physician and remained at Ince's side until that afternoon, when Ince's wife arrived to take the sick man home.

The San Diego District Attorney closed the case without further investigation. Although there would be no further investigation of Ince's untimely death, some very peculiar events transpired immediately after the group's return to Los Angeles. Gossip columnist Louella Parsons was given a lifetime contract with Hearst and expanded publication. Ince's wife refused an autopsy of her husband's body and had him cremated immediately after a brief service. A trust fund was set up for Ince's wife, and the apartment was mysteriously paid off, but she never lived there again. Marion Davies claimed that neither Charlie Chaplin nor Louella Parsons were onboard that weekend, even though several studio people claimed to have seen them all leave together in the same vehicle.

Was this a case of the rich getting away with murder? D. W. Griffith claimed in later years, "All you have to do to make Hearst turn white as a ghost is to mention Ince's name. There's plenty wrong there, but Hearst is too big to touch."

THELMA TODD

Best known as "The Ice Cream Blonde," Thelma Todd came to Hollywood after winning the title of Miss Massachusetts in 1925. A talent scout noticed her and offered her a contract with Paramount Pictures. She began acting in short feature films, mostly in bit parts and background. In 1927, Todd was offered her first feature role in the film "Fascinating Youth." Her career steadily climbed, and she made over one hundred pictures during her career to enormous success. She was best known for her roles in the Marx Brothers pictures "Monkey Business" and "Horse Feathers."

Producer Roland West, a married man with whom Todd had been having an affair for some time, advised her to cash in on her fame and open a restaurant. She took his advice and opened Thelma Todd's Sidewalk Cafe in Pacific Palisades. The venture was a huge success, patronized by both celebrities and notorious underworld criminals.

Enjoying the nightlife, Todd frequented the lavish nightclubs in the Hollywood area. After an evening at the Trocadero Restaurant on Sunset Boulevard, Todd's chauffer drove her back to her home above her restaurant. The next morning, her body was found in the garage, and another Hollywood scandal was born.

Todd's maid began her duties that morning and discovered her employer was not in the house. She checked the garage to see if the car was there and found Todd slumped over in the vehicle, still in the gown she had been wearing the night before. The maid testified that she had seen blood on her clothing and face. An autopsy later proved that Todd's blood alcohol level was .13, and her blood contained a seventy-five percent carbon monoxide level.

The scene appeared to the police to be a suicide with no signs of a struggle. A Grand Jury investigation ruled the death carbon monoxide poisoning, but the evidence of blood on her skin and clothing went without answer.

Another discrepancy in the case was testimony from West's wife, claiming she had seen Todd that morning driving through the intersection of Hollywood and Vine in her Packard convertible. A later investigation of West caused him to admit to police that on the evening in question, he and Todd had an argument in which he pushed her out of her apartment. She screamed and pounded on the door. The police would confirm that fresh nicks were evident on the door.

The attorney for Todd demanded a second investigation, convinced that his client was murdered by crime boss Lucky Luciano, who had approached Todd about opening an illegal gambling establishment in the upstairs apartment and promoting clientele from her celebrity friends. Refusing his offer was compared to signing her own death warrant. The attorney was later advised to drop the case by none other than producer Hal Roach.

Another rumor whispered around Hollywood involved her lover Roland West himself. Some claim he had been trying to break off the relationship with Todd for some time and staged the fight with a look-alike to make it appear she was distraught. He then rendered Todd unconscious, placed her in the car, and started the motor. After the scandal, he never worked in pictures again.

The funeral for Thelma Todd read like a 'Who's Who of Hollywood.' Todd was laid out in a casket draped with yellow roses. Her skin color was that of the peaches and cream she portrayed on screen. Friend Zazu Pitts claimed, "She looked like she was going to sit up and talk." After the star-studded funeral, Todd's body was cremated and shipped to her hometown of Lawrence, Massachusetts. Her remains were placed in the casket with her mother when she passed away, and they were buried together.

Some years later, in 1953, Roland West confessed to the murder of Thelma Todd, stating that he had been trying to stop her from going out again that evening. However, no charges were ever filed against him.

Benjamin "Bugsy" Siegel

Known as one of the greatest underworld crime figures of the twentieth century, Benjamin "Bugsy" Siegel came up through the ranks of the crime world with boyhood friend, George Raft, who later became a movie star.

Living and working in Chicago, Siegel was sent out west with some of his associates to start business in Hollywood. He came to town and began infiltrating the Hollywood social scene. Renting a mansion, he began dating known party-giver Countess Dorothy Taylor Di Frasso. They dated for a short while, but neither wanted to be tied to the other. Siegel was introduced to Jean Harlow through an invitation from her stepfather. While Harlow did not accept his invitations, he did appear at her funeral years later.

He found working in Hollywood very lucrative, making money in shady deals with the studio big shots as well as the small players.

The crypt of Benjamin "Bugsy" Siegel is located at the Temple Beth Olam Mausoleum in Hollywood, California.

Despite his reputation, he began living like a celebrity, hobnobbing with greats like Clark Gable, Cary Grant, and Gary Cooper. Siegel dated socialites and unknowns alike. During one short stint in jail, he was released long enough to enjoy the company of then-girlfriend Wendy Barrie.

Upon his release from jail on a trumped-up charge of murdering associate Harry Greenberg, he met and started dating Virginia Hill, a notorious gold-digger who had moved west from New York, where she had dated Lucky Luciano. She dated only wealthy men and later had difficulty with the IRS when she claimed her $500,000-dollar-a-year income came from ardent admirers. Siegel was often seen escorting her to movie premieres and parties.

During this time, Siegel decided to move to Las Vegas to build a lavish new casino. He convinced many of his mafia friends to invest in the Flamingo Hotel and Casino in this burgeoning Mecca, but the progress was slow and went far over budget.

On June 20, 1947, Siegel arrived at the mansion of Virginia Hill, who had left that morning for Europe. He had agreed to watch her home during her absence and invited long-time friend Al Smiley to visit that day. The two men were relaxing in the living room, Siegel sitting next to the large French windows looking out over the front yard. Without warning, four bullets shot through the glass, two hitting him in the head and two entering his body, killing Siegel where he sat. Neighbors testified later that they heard a car speed away from the house immediately after the shots were fired.

Virginia Hill made only this statement upon hearing of the dead in her home, "It looks so bad to have a thing like that happen in your house." A police investigation was inconclusive, and no arrests were made. Was it a rival crime boss wanting Siegel out of the way? Perhaps angry investors in the Las Vegas project that left them out thousands of dollars? Did Virginia Hill play a part in the murder of her boyfriend?

Time magazine summed up the events: "Where the truth was, no one seemed to know or care, but a wonderful time was had by all."

The funeral for the notorious gangster was attended by only five members of his family. Self-proclaimed friends and the Hollywood elite chose to avoid the memorial.

George Reeves

Another of the cast of "Gone with the Wind" to take his life would be handsome George Reeves, who played Stuart Tarlton in the opening sequences of the Civil War drama.

Reeves began his career with this small part and worked sporadically after "Gone with the Wind," but his career would not take off until he was offered the role of 'The Man of Steel' in "The Adventures of Superman" in the early 1950s. It is rumored that George hesitated to take the role until persuaded by his mistress, Toni Mannix, wife of Eddie "Bulldog" Mannix. Reeves would find the fame he sought with "The Adventures of Superman," appearing in over one hundred episodes, doing endorsements for Kellogg's Frosted Flakes, and making public appearances as Superman across the country.

Soon Reeves found that he was being typecast in the superhero role, and other acting jobs dried up for the actor. It is said that the lack of more challenging roles created depression for Reeves.

In 1958, Reeves ended his relationship with Toni Mannix and, allegedly, she did not take the news well, harassing him after the breakup. Reeves met Lenore Lemmon during this time, and soon the two were engaged.

On the evening of June 15, 1959, Reeves, fiancée Lemmon, and friend George Condon spent the evening drinking in Reeves' home and then went to bed. In the early hours of June 16, they were awakened by Carol Van Ronkel and William Bliss, who came to visit. Reeves became infuriated with the couple, and his last words to the group were "I'm tired. I'm going back to bed." Lemmon, somewhat amused by the behavior, commented to their friends, "He'll probably go up to his room and shoot himself." Around 1:20 a.m., the small gathering heard one shot fired and ran upstairs to see what created that loud bang. They found Reeves lying on the bed, naked, with a .30-caliber pistol next to his still body.

While the death of George Reeves has officially been declared a suicide, rumors have circulated since the death that it was in fact not suicide, but murder. Why do you ask? Let's look at the evidence. Some say he had been receiving death threats in the months leading up to the fateful night. His longtime lover, Toni Mannix, had connections to the mafia, but then so did his fiancée. The group that found his body did not call the police until forty-five minutes after the shot had been fired and told police investigators they heard only the one shot. Police detectives found three bullet holes, one in the ceiling and two more in the floorboards. One bullet casing was found underneath the body of the actor and no fingerprints were on the gun. Later, the story of the bullet in the ceiling would be explained by a close friend of Lemmon's, who claimed her girlfriend fired into the ceiling to "show what the gun sounded like." Raising even more suspicions would be Lemmon's disappearance the next day. She never returned to California.

The funeral was held July 1, 1959, at Wayside Chapel of the Gates Funeral Home in Los Angeles. The Reverend R. Parker Jones remembered the actor's "selfless interest in the service of the lives of children, especially those in hospitals."

After the memorial service, Reeves' body was temporarily entombed in Woodlawn Mausoleum until he could be transported back to Cincinnati for cremation. Finally, on February 10, 1960, the body was cremated and re-interred in the final resting place.

Suicide or murder? The myths have continued for over forty years, with those involved long since in silence. Will we ever really know what brought the Man of Steel to his final rest?

NATALIE WOOD

One of the most questionable deaths in Hollywood history — the case of Natalie Wood — remains a mystery to this day. What really happened to the doe-eyed brunette whose life mirrored the dramatic parts she played on screen?

Natalie Wood was born to immigrant parents who fled Russia to settle in San Francisco. Wood's mother was reportedly overbearing, some even referring to her as insane. Her father was no comfort to the young girl either, drinking heavily during most of her childhood.

At the age of four, Wood was cast as an extra in the production "Happy Land." Living vicariously through her daughter, Wood's mother decided her daughter would become a movie star and moved

The headstone of Natalie Wood as it appears at Pierce Brothers Westwood Memorial Park in Westwood, California.

the family to Los Angeles. Wood struggled for roles, but finally was awarded a part in the 1946 film "Tomorrow Is Forever." The next year, Wood found success with small roles in "The Ghost and Mrs. Muir" and her most memorable childhood film, "Miracle on 34th Street."

In 1959, Wood was on the set of "The Star," costarring Bette Davis, when the script called for her to dive into the dark, murky water. Wood was terrified of the water, stating she could swim only a little. The director told the young girl that a double would be used for the scene, but changed his mind at the last minute, causing Wood to go into hysterics. It was only after Davis intervened on her behalf that a double was used during the filming.

The transition from child actor to adult is difficult at best, but Wood eased into her teenage years, winning a lead in the film "Rebel Without a Cause" with James Dean, Sal Mineo, and Nick Adams, all of whom would later die mysteriously. Director Nicholas Ray took a personal interest in the young actress, and the two began a torrid affair, Ray being twenty-five years her senior. Wood was nominated for an Academy Award for Best Supporting Actress for her work in this film.

It was later that year that she would meet Rock and Roll idol Elvis Presley, and the two began dating. Wood's only statement about dating the king was, "Elvis was so square, we'd go...for hot fudge sundaes. He didn't drink, he didn't swear, he didn't even smoke. It was like having the date that I never had in high school." It was rumored that the two wanted to marry, but Presley's mother did not like Wood and ended the relationship.

Soon after her eighteenth birthday in 1957, Wood met and married fellow actor Robert Wagner. The two were very much in love, but Wood's film schedule kept her busy for most of the early part of their marriage, causing strain to the newly married couple. A brief affair with costar Warren Beatty during the filming of "Splendor in the Grass" fueled the difficulties in the marriage. The couple divorced in 1962.

The early 1960s proved very profitable for Wood with parts in hit films like "West Side Story," "Gypsy," and "Proper Stranger," for which she received her second Academy Award nomination. In the late 1960s, Wood's career began to slide until she appeared in the 1969 production of "Bob and Carol and Ted and Alice," which garnered her critical acclaim.

Wood married again in 1969, to British producer Richard Gregson, and the two had a child together. This union, however, was short-lived; they divorced within a couple of years after Wood found out Gregson was having an affair.

By 1972, she and first husband Robert Wagner had reconciled and remarried. They had a child, and Wood decided to retire from show business. When asked later about their early relationship, she claimed, "We were both scared, insecure," and believed people who told them that the marriage wouldn't work.

It would not be until 1979 that Wood would work again, taking a part on the television series "From Here to Eternity," for which she won a Golden Globe. Coupled with Wagner's success on the series "Hart to Hart," the couple seemed to be happy.

On Thanksgiving weekend 1981, Wood, Wagner, and actor Christopher Walken boarded Wagner's yacht, the *Splendour*, in Marina Del Rey. The small party headed to Catalina Island for the holiday. On the surface, the group seemed happy and festive, but underneath there was an air of tension permeating the entourage. Wood was feeling insecure and jealous of her husband's relationship with costar Stephanie Powers. Wagner had been spending much of his time with the redhead after receiving news that her past lover William Holden had died suddenly. The producers halted production to give Powers time to grieve, and Wagner's attempts to comfort Powers caused Wood distress. It was also rumored that Woods and Walken had been carrying on a flirtation that was blossoming into a romance during their work together. The alcohol flowed freely during the trip, fueling the fire.

On Saturday afternoon, the trio headed ashore for dinner, drinking heavily during the meal. Witnesses claimed to hear the couple arguing at the table and Wood overtly flirting with Walken. At the conclusion of the meal, the group boarded the dinghy and headed back to the boat. They continued drinking after the captain of the vessel retired for the night. Around midnight, Wood said she was going below to change clothes.

Approximately thirty minutes later, the captain made his last round for the night, noticed the dinghy missing, and reported this to Wagner, who went to check on his wife and discovered her missing from the bedroom. He immediately called the police and Coast Guard to assist in searching for his missing wife. The search went on through the night without success.

At 7:44 a.m. on Sunday, November 29, 1981, the body of Natalie Wood — dressed in her nightgown, socks, and a water-soaked down jacket — was found floating face down in the water. Speculation was that she had decided to go ashore or take the dinghy to look at the stars, slipped on the wet surface, hit her head, and fell into the icy water. This would be an unusual occurrence, but in her drunken state, she would have impaired judgment. Her hands and wrists appeared to have scratches, indicating she attempted to climb on the rocks before drowning. After an autopsy, the death was ruled accidental, but the coroner stated, "There is room for further investigation."

A witness came forward soon after, stating that she had been aboard a boat moored one hundred yards from Wagner's yacht. She heard a woman's voice call out for help around midnight and a male voice respond that he was coming to get her. There was silence after the exchange, so the woman assumed everything was all right.

Speculation continued to swirl around the death. It was well-known that Wood had a fear of water, so why would she go out at night, alone, to tempt fate? Wood's body was transported to Westwood Memorial Village to be prepared for the funeral. According to those who witnessed the condition of Wood's body, she was in no condition to have an open casket, but makeup artists from MGM would be sent over to take care of making her presentable. She was dressed in a fox fur stole Wagner had purchased to give to his wife, but never had the opportunity. Her daughter asked that her diamond earrings be placed on her prior to the service.

Natalie Wood lay in state in the chapel on December 2, 1981, a blanket of gardenias covering her casket. Close friends Roddy McDowall, Hope Lange, and Tommy Thompson each gave a tearful eulogy. At the end of the service, which was attended by one hundred of Wood's close friends and family, Wagner bent over his wife and kissed her one last time. The pallbearers carrying her casket included Gregory Peck, Laurence Olivier, Frank Sinatra, and Fred Astaire.

Natalie Wood was buried in a small plot of land at Westwood Memorial Park, a simple bronze plate with the name Natalie Wood Wagner marking her grave.

BOB CRANE

Bob Crane, the resourceful colonel on the hit television show "Hogan's Heroes," left a legacy not for his television and stage appearances, but for his unsolved brutal murder and a hidden, secret life unknown to the world until after his death.

Bob Crane had aspirations to perform in front of an audience since childhood. An avid musician, he excelled at percussion instruments and performed for two years with the Connecticut Symphony Orchestra as a teenager. He traveled with various bands as a drummer before settling as a disc jockey in Hornell, New York.

He excelled on the radio, hosting his own show for six years on WICC in Bridgeport, Connecticut. He married and settled down, but Crane's ambition called for him to do bigger things with his life.

Headstone of Bob Crane and his wife Sigrid Valdis at Pierce Brothers Westwood Memorial Park in Westwood, California.

Crane moved his family to Los Angeles and took a job with KNX AM radio as a celebrity interviewer. His entertaining banter and sharp wit charmed audiences, and he became the highest-paid jockey on the air, earning $100,000 annually.

Still not satisfied, Crane wanted to break into acting, telling a friend, "I want to be the next Jack Lemmon." In between his radio assignments, Crane guest-starred in the films "Mantrap" and "Peyton Place" and worked his way up to interim host for the daytime game show "Who Do You Trust?", filling in for Johnny Carson.

In 1963, after an appearance on "The Dick Van Dyke Show," Crane was offered a part on "The Donna Reed Show" as the next-door neighbor. He gladly took the role and lasted two years with the show.

Producers offered Crane a part in the upcoming new series "Hogan's Heroes" as the title character. He jumped at the chance, and the six-year series would become his most-loved project.

In 1970, Crane divorced his first wife and married actress Patricia Olsen, his costar on the series. The couple enjoyed great success together until the show's end in 1971.

After playing Hogan, Crane felt he was primed for much better parts and turned down several good offers. He took various guest star roles while waiting for his next big offer. Offers for sitcom pilots came across his desk, but he turned them all down.

In 1974, Crane received an offer of $300,000 a year for his own radio show, but settled on doing his own television show, "The Bob Crane Show," instead. The show bombed with audiences and critics, lasting only two months before it was canceled. By now, Crane struggled to find any work, having rejected most of the television producers. He was left to do guest spots on "The Love Boat," which was known in the industry as career poison.

By the late 1970s, Crane was working steadily, performing in dinner theaters across the country. He had purchased the rights to the play "Beginners Luck," taking the production to dozens of cities.

On June 28, 1978, Crane had just finished performing at the Windmill Dinner Theater in Scottsdale, Arizona. He was staying at the Winfield Apartment-Hotel during the run of the show and returned there with video equipment salesman John Carpenter, who had been introduced to Crane by "Hogan's Heroes" costar Richard Dawson, and the two had developed a working relationship.

Later that evening, the two men went to a local bar for drinks and met two women. At 2 a.m., the group went to the Safari Coffee Shop and then returned to the hotel. Sometime during the evening, Crane announced to Carpenter that he had decided to change his lifestyle and cut off relations with people like Carpenter, thereby ending the friendship. Supposedly, Carpenter went back to his hotel to pack and head for California.

The next day, cast member Victoria Berry arrived at the hotel to check on the actor when he did not arrive for the cast luncheon that afternoon. The door to his suite was ajar, very unusual for Crane since he always used two locks on every door. When Berry pushed the door open, she saw two bottles of liquor on the table, one empty and one half empty. She called out to Crane, but received no answer. Crossing the room, she opened the bedroom door and found Crane dead on the bed.

The actor, clad only in his underwear, was unrecognizable. Someone had beaten him about the face and head, and the bed was soaked with blood. An electrical cord was wrapped around his neck. The only way the actress could identify her costar was by the wristwatch he always wore. She began to scream, summoning other guests to the crime scene.

The police arrived and, based on the evidence found, determined that the killer was known to Crane and must have been in the room prior to the murder and left an unlocked window or door to ensure easy access to the room later. Crane appeared to have been asleep on his right side when the attacker struck him on the left side of his head. The second hit shattered his skull. The electrical cord had been fastened around his neck post-mortem. Evidence showed that the killer then wiped the blood from the weapon on the bed sheet and pulled the sheet over Crane's head before leaving.

Further investigation ruled out robbery. Crane's wallet was in the room with all of his money still there. More disturbing to investigators was the large collection of pornographic material found in the room with Crane. Unknown to the public, he had a compulsion for lewd sexual acts, videotaping himself with various sex partners, and developing still photos in the makeshift bathroom darkroom. The detectives cataloged more than fifty tapes of Crane and various women, along with negatives of women both partially clothed and nude.

Upon their search of Crane's black camera bag, which he always carried with him, police noticed several items were missing. This bag was taken into evidence, but later mysteriously disappeared...never to be seen again.

The prime suspect was John Carpenter, the last man to see Crane alive. Carpenter called the hotel several times and appeared unsurprised when the police picked up the phone. The car Carpenter had rented was impounded and blood was found on the interior matching Crane's blood type. Since this was before the advent of DNA evidence, they had no way of proving conclusively this was Crane's blood.

Without sufficient evidence, the police could not arrest John Carpenter, and he was freed. The lifestyle Crane enjoyed led investigators to believe the murderer could have been any number of people wanting him dead — from jealous husbands to jealous girlfriends.

Crane's body was flown back to California for an elaborate funeral on July 5, 1978. The service at St. Paul the Apostle Catholic Church in Westwood was attended by television stars Patty Duke, Carroll O'Connor, and John Astin. The starring cast of "Hogan's Heroes" were the pallbearers, carrying the remains of their beloved colonel to his resting place at Oakwood Memorial Park in Chatsworth, California.

Even in death, Bob Crane would not rest. Twenty years later, his widow would move his remains to the exclusive Westwood Memorial Park, where he was again laid to rest beneath an elaborate headstone.

Fourteen years after the death of Crane, police arrested John Carpenter for his murder, claiming they had found brain tissue within the rental car and tested it for DNA. The evidence was inconclusive, and Carpenter was set free after his indictment. He was proven innocent and died in 1998.

Although the death of one of the most-loved television characters has never been solved, the funnyman will live on as Colonel Hogan.

Chapter Three:

THOSE WHO LEFT US TOO SOON

It seems the lives of the young, up-and-coming movie stars intrigue us the most. We watch them begin their careers and let them climb their way into our hearts with stellar performances while waiting for the next great performance from the new cream of Hollywood actors and actresses. When one of these children of the screen is taken from us far too early, it creates a loss in all of us greater than the loss of those who celebrated a long life. We will never have the opportunity to see the next performance on film; instead, we will look back on the start of a brilliant career cut short.

RUDOLPH VALENTINO

Rudolph Valentino, the legendary Latin lover who personified the smoldering lover on screen, began his career as a dancer after coming to the United States in 1913. After teaching dance from 1914 through 1916, Valentino moved out West and began his movie career with bit parts, including a very small part in the film "Alimony" in 1917. Valentino would land his first major role in 1921, when director Rex Ingram cast him in the epic film "The Four Horsemen of the Apocalypse." Later that same year, Valentino was cast in the classic "The Sheik," a film that rocketed him to mega stardom and creating the sexual creature women swooned over.

While Valentino would have great success on the screen, his personal life was anything but the picture-perfect romance he personified. He met actress Jean Acker in 1919, and the two married November 5, 1919. It is rumored that on the wedding night, Acker locked herself in the bedroom of the honeymoon suite, not allowing Valentino access, saying the marriage was a "horrible mistake."

While some claimed the marriage was never consummated, the two remained married until March 1923, when they finally divorced. Within two weeks of his divorce from Acker, Valentino married actress Natacha Rambova, but she became a hindrance to his career, trying to manage his films and public appearances. When Valentino signed a contract with Paramount, Adolph Zukor put in a clause stating that his wife was banned from any movie set Valentino was working on. Rambova ordered Valentino to leave Paramount and attempted to produce the film "The Hooded Falcon" for him. Ending up a huge financial disaster, the film was never completed.

By 1925, Valentino was the biggest box office draw, beating out many of the most famous contemporaries of the day. He starred in "Son of the Sheik" that year, and some maintain this was his best work ever on the screen.

During this time, Valentino suffered ill health, complaining of severe stomach pains. Nevertheless, he embarked on a publicity tour and traveled to New York, but upon his arrival, he was in need of medical care. Valentino checked into Polyclinic Hospital August 16,

Artist rendering of Rudolph Valentino in his casket. *Courtesy of Todd Wiesenhutter.*

The author in front of Rudolph Valentino's crypt in the Cathedral
Mausoleum at Hollywood Forever Cemetery in Los Angeles.

1926, and was found to have gastric ulcers brought on by the stress
of his lifestyle. The tabloid news claimed that he was in fact a "pink
powder puff," an outright affront to his manhood. X-rays confirmed
he had a perforated ulcer. Some claim he was also suffering from a
ruptured appendix, contributing to his condition. He was rushed
into surgery, but it would be too late for the cinema idol. Uremic
poisoning had already begun to spread throughout his body. On
August 21, Valentino stated he felt better and was looking forward
to a quiet vacation upon his recovery. Unfortunately, that afternoon
his fever rose to 104 degrees, and the pain became so severe that
morphine was given to ease his discomfort.

On August 23, Joseph Schneck, chairman of United Artists,
visited Valentino; he was not looking well, but despite his condition,
Valentino told Schneck, "Don't worry, chief. I will be all right." By
that evening, he was barely conscious, and news had spread that the
matinee idol was ill. Thousands of fans crowded the streets outside
the hospital, awaiting news of his condition. Alas, the great lover

of the screen would not get better. His fever continuing to spike, causing the gravely ill Valentino to lapse into a coma. His boyhood priest administered last rites and, at 12:10 p.m. on August 23, 1926, Rudolph Valentino was dead at the age of thirty-one.

Upon hearing of Valentino's death, the crowd outside the hospital became so riotous that the police had to be called to restore order. The hospital staff placed Valentino's body in a plain wicker casket and carried it out of the hospital without notice. A nondescript van transported his body to the Campbell Funeral Parlor on 66th Street to be prepared.

When Silent Screen actress Pola Negri was notified of the sudden demise of Valentino, she took to her bed, making sure the press was given moment-to-moment updates as to her mental health and travel arrangements to attend the funeral. She claimed that Valentino had proposed to her and that the two had been making plans to marry. It was questioned whether this was true or just a publicity stunt, since Valentino never spoke of this to anyone.

The following day, on August 24th, the crowds outside the mortuary were swelling and many people were injured. The visitation would begin that afternoon, with over 10,000 people waiting on the street. At 2 p.m., the doors of the mortuary opened, and the crowd surged ahead with such force that police were pushed through the plate glass window in front of the building. Backup was called to quiet the surly crowd, who desperately wanted one last glimpse of the great actor. Medical personnel set up a makeshift first-aid station to care for those who were injured during the stampede.

Movie fans, in their desperation, snatched up souvenirs from the funeral home — anything that wasn't nailed down was stolen. An attempt was made to move the body to one of the smaller rooms to better control the flow of visitors. Several women reportedly fainted upon seeing their idol lying in the bronze and silver casket.

After the doors closed, several guards stood watch over the body. They claimed to be ordered by none other than Mussolini, but later this was found out to be a publicity stunt. The next morning, Valentino's manager canceled the additional public viewing, allowing only family and friends access to the room. Pola Negri arrived on the scene and fainted upon seeing her beloved. She alternated between crying and swooning, always within eye of the cameras and reporters and seemingly on cue.

By August 26, over two hundred police were staged on the street. The private viewing had been held over, allowing time for Valentino's brother to arrive from Italy. At midnight, the coffin was closed for the last time and made ready for Valentino's final journey to California.

On August 30, the procession for Rudolph Valentino commenced, leaving the funeral home at 10:48 a.m. with 6,000 fans and admirers looking on.

Along the route to Los Angeles, the train carrying Valentino's remains stopped in Chicago for a public viewing before continuing the journey. Upon arrival in Hollywood, an invitation-only memorial service was scheduled for five hundred guests, including Mary Pickford, Douglas Fairbanks, Clifton Webb, Gloria Swanson, and Harry Houdini. The funeral was something out of a movie script. Soloists from Chicago Opera Company—along with a full choir—performed. Chopin's Funeral March was played as the casket was escorted to the waiting funeral coach.

However, despite his legend status and highly publicized marriage, little was known about the one woman whose death devastated Valentino and haunted him for the rest of his life: Virginia Richdale Kerrigan was the daughter of Nina Richdale and William Wallace Kerrigan. A friend, William Kerrigan eventually became Valentino's manager. Valentino had met little Virginia through her father and became very attached to the little girl. Valentino had a fondness for all children, but Virginia stole his heart away. He would visit their home often and take Virginia for rides through Hollywood.

It was during the Christmas season of 1924 that Virginia and her parents were attending a party, and Virginia wore the new dress she had been given for Christmas. In the 1920s, gas heaters would warm the houses, usually with an open flame, and little Virginia danced too close to the fire in her new dress. The material caught flame and she was engulfed in a matter of moments. The family rushed her to the hospital, but she would suffer for the next thirty-six hours before passing on December 27, 1924.

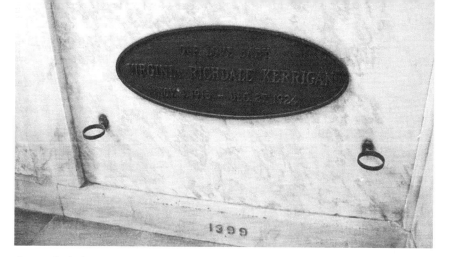

Crypt of Virginia Richdale Kerrigan at Hollywood Forever Cemetery in Hollywood, California, is also located near Valentino's. Valentino was quite devastated by the young girl's death.

Valentino was devastated by the news of the child's passing. His profound love of Virginia made the event almost unbearable. According to accounts from Virginia's brother, Patrick O. Kerrigan, who would be born after her passing, Valentino would visit the site regularly, leaving flowers for the child.

As fate would have it, at the time of Valentino's untimely death, the family had no money for a burial space to inter him, so June Mathis, who wrote the screenplay "The Four Horsemen," Valentino's first feature role, allowed his body to be placed in one of the crypts she had purchased for her family. The crypt is not only within the same mausoleum, but also within a few feet of Virginia's crypt. Plans at the time were to move Valentino's body to a memorial fitting such a great star, but this would never come to pass. At the time of June Mathis' passing, it was decided that Valentino would remain where he was permanently.

On the first anniversary of Valentino's death, a mysterious lady in black placed roses at the crypt, but never spoke of who she was to anyone. She continued this practice annually, finally revealing her identity years later. She claimed that when she was a young girl Valentino had visited her in the hospital. She was gravely ill, but the star's kind words and reassurance that she would outlive him kept her spirits high. His only request of the girl was to remember him, and she kept her promise.

ELVIS PRESLEY

The life of the great King of Rock and Roll is known the world over. From his humble beginnings in Tupelo, Mississippi, to his meteoric climb to the heights of success and marriage to the beautiful Priscilla Beaulieu, Elvis Presley's life is an open book and has been a forum of public discussion for decades.

But how much do people really know about the private health and last moments of his life? After years of drug abuse in increasing quantities and strength, Presley's health had deteriorated, but he continued to push on. At the time of his death, he was planning a new tour, the second that year, with the help of the ever-present Colonel Tom Parker.

On the morning of August 15, 1977, Presley and his bodyguards, dubbed the Memphis Mafia, were taking care of last-minute details prior to the tour commencing. Presley was known for spending much of his day behind closed doors in his grand master suite on the second floor of his home, Graceland. After spending time alone with his girlfriend, Ginger Alden, he finally emerged from the room late in the afternoon and went to the dentist's office to acquire more prescription drugs with his cousin Billy Smith, Billy's wife, and Ginger. His drug addiction had escalated to include narcotics like Demerol and Dilaudid, which are often prescribed to cancer patients. This, coupled with his southern-fried diet, caused obesity and severe health issues.

That evening, Presley spent time with the Memphis Mafia, playing racquetball and then singing while accompanied on the piano. He arrived back home and prepared to go to bed. At 6 a.m. on August 16, Presley went to the bathroom to sit in his barber chair to read, an activity he performed regularly when he was restless. At 2 p.m., Alden awoke to an empty bed and walked to the bathroom door and knocked. When there was no answer, she opened the door and found Presley unconscious on the floor. She called downstairs and requested assistance from the maid.

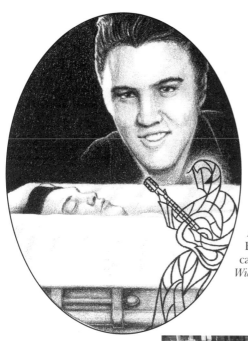

Artist rendering of Elvis Presley in his casket. *Courtesy of Todd Wiesenhutter.*

A view of Elvis Presley's gravesite at Graceland. *Courtesy of Kyle Kesselring.*

Several of his assistants ran upstairs and entered the bathroom. They rolled Presley's body over, and it was apparent that the king was dead. They contacted the local hospital, and an ambulance arrived to take him to Baptist Hospital in Memphis. Within thirty minutes of Presley's arrival at the hospital, the doctor pronounced him dead. An announcement was made at the hospital, and the news created worldwide grief. Hordes of people converged on Memphis. Hotels and flights were booked to capacity. Fans lined up outside the gates of Graceland, hoping to have one last glimpse of their favorite rock star as his body returned to his home. Police and the National Guard were called in to assist with keeping public peace during this tragic time.

An autopsy was performed; the cause of death was determined to be a heart attack caused by cardiac arrhythmia. His personal hairdresser, Larry, came to style the king's hair one last time. In a 2005 interview, he described the scene at the mortuary upon seeing the body of Presley with a sheet covering him. He stood above the body in silence, taking in the realization that his long-time friend was gone. He touched up the roots of Presley's coal-black hair and spent another forty-five minutes preparing the king's hair to perfection.

On August 17, fans continued to converge at Graceland, waiting for the public viewing. Authorities struggled to keep fans from scaling the walls or climbing the gates. Finally, the police announced that Graceland would be closed to the public unless the crowds calmed down. The public viewing began at 3 p.m. that afternoon in the foyer of Graceland. There was to be only a two-hour period of visitation, but this would not be sufficient for the enormous crowd that had gathered, so the hours were extended to 6:30. Though there were more than 100,000 people waiting in line, only 25,000 actually got in to see the King of Rock and Roll that day. However, the crowd continued its vigil outside the gates all through the night and into the next day.

A private funeral was held at Graceland on August 18, 1977, for the family, including ex-wife Priscilla Presley, and invited guests, such as Anne Margaret, George Hamilton, and Chet Atkins. Presley, dressed in a blue suit his father had given him for Christmas, was lying in state at the front of the room in a copper casket. Dozens of flower arrangements filled the room as the Reverend C. W. Bradley began the service. The Stamps Quartet, Presley's backup group, performed several of his favorite gospel hymns.

At the conclusion of the service, ten pallbearers carried the nine-hundred-pound casket out the front doors of his home to the waiting funeral coach. As they walked down the steps of the large front porch, suddenly a limb broke off of a nearby tree. One pallbearer made the comment, "He's still at work," as they continued down the walk.

The funeral procession included forty-nine cars behind the white Cadillac hearse carrying Presley's body. They arrived at Forest Hill Cemetery for another private service in the mausoleum chapel where Presley's father, Vernon, would kiss his son's rose-covered casket for the last time. With that, Presley was entombed in the same private mausoleum as his mother, Grace, and the gates closed.

This, however, would not be the final resting place for Elvis Presley for very long.

On the evening of August 30, three men broke into the cemetery with plans to steal the "king's" corpse for the purposes of ransoming the body. Shortly after midnight, the men arrived on the scene, but the police had received an anonymous tip that afternoon revealing the plans. They laid in wait and apprehended the men as they approached the Presley crypt. The men attempted to escape on foot without success. They were sentenced to a minimum stay in jail, but the Presley family realized that Presley's remains would not be safe on such public display.

On October 3, the remains of both Elvis Presley and his mother were removed from Forest Hill Cemetery and laid to rest in the Prayer Garden Chapel on the south side of his estate Graceland, where he still resides today.

GRACE KELLY

One of the most beautiful faces ever to grace the silver screen, Grace Kelly began her acting career in college, knowing early on that she wanted to become an actress. Her family begrudgingly agreed, and she attended the American Academy of Dramatic Arts. Upon graduating, she began acting and found herself on the Broadway stage in 1949 in "The Father," playing opposite Raymond Massey.

Kelly soon embarked on a cross-country journey to Hollywood, where she almost immediately became a star, acting opposite Gary Cooper in the film "High Noon" in 1952. She and Cooper would have a heated affair during filming and continued seeing each other into the next year. Kelly's next film, "Mogambo," in 1953, launched the talented actress as a full-fledged movie star. She continued acting and would have affairs with several of her costars, including Clark Gable and Ray Milland. She was given the lead role in Alfred Hitchcock's "Dial M for Murder" and would cement a long, successful career with the director. Her role in "The Country Girl" would win her an Academy Award in 1954 for Best Actress.

In 1955, Kelly attended the Cannes Film Festival in France and was introduced to Prince Rainier of Monaco. The two became infatuated with each other, and the prince would travel to the United States to propose marriage within a few months of their meeting. They were married in a grand ceremony on April 18, 1956, at the Catholic Cathedral of St. Nicholas in Monaco as the world watched in awe. It was truly a fairy tale come true: American girl turns actress...and then becomes a princess. She had her first two children, Caroline and Albert, and much later, after several miscarriages, she gave birth to Princess Stephanie in 1965.

Kelly performed charitable work and served on the board of 20th Century Fox. She desperately wanted to go back to her acting, but the royal family would not allow it. By the mid 1970s, she began keeping her own apartment in Paris, as rumors traveled about difficulties in the marriage.

Artist rendering of Grace Kelly in her casket by Todd Wiesenhutter.

On the afternoon of September 14, 1982, Kelly and her youngest daughter were traveling home from a day at the dressmaker's. Kelly was negotiating the winding road Moyenne Corniche when she lost control of the car and careened down the steep cliff. Mother and daughter were rushed to the local hospital, where Princess Grace was diagnosed with a brain hemorrhage, a collapsed lung, and a broken leg. It was also determined she had suffered a stroke, which had caused her to lose control of the automobile. The next day, the family agreed to remove her from life support, and the film-actress-turned-princess was dead at the age of fifty-three.

After her death, Kelly was taken from the hospital to the family residence and placed in the Palatine Chapel. On September 15, the public would be allowed visitation, an opportunity to see the beautiful princess in her white-silk-lined casket, dressed in a gown of white, clutching her rosary.

The funeral mass was set for September 18 and commenced with a fanfare of bugles announcing the procession through the streets of Monaco, which were lined with adoring subjects as twenty pallbearers carried the casket to the Cathedral of St. Nicholas. The procession arrived at the same chapel where the prince and his bride had exchanged wedding vows more than twenty years earlier. Prince Rainier wept openly as the Archbishop delivered the service. Eight hundred guests crowded the chapel, including Barbara Sinatra, Princess Diana, Nancy Reagan, and Cary Grant. Princess Grace of Monaco was entombed within the family mausoleum beneath the floor of the chapel in which she had been married.

MARILYN MONROE

There are very few celebrity lives more well-known or extensively documented than the life of the immortal Marilyn Monroe. Her life began with tragedy and ended cloaked in mystery and intrigue. Many questions continue to surround the untimely death of the actress. Was it murder or suicide that took this movie star and turned her into a goddess for all time?

It was widely known that Monroe was a temperamental actress with long bouts of depression resulting from a lifetime of tragedy. Yet she always seemed to be the survivor, continuing to be loved by her fans and adoring men. After three failed marriages and several miscarriages that rendered her alone once again, Monroe continued a power struggle with 20th Century Fox and was released from her latest picture, "Something's Got to Give."

The crypt of Marilyn Monroe is at Pierce Brothers Westwood Memorial Park in Westwood, California.

It was the evening of August 4, 1962, when Monroe spoke to her devoted housekeeper, Eunice Murray. Just before retiring for the evening, she told Murray, "I think we'll go to the beach tomorrow for a ride" and closed the bedroom door. These would be the last words Marilyn Monroe would ever speak.

Murray awoke sometime around 10 p.m. and went to the bedroom door to check on her employer. When she did not receive a response, which was not unusual, she went to the garden window and peered in. She witnessed Monroe's nude body draped over the bed, unconscious. She ran to the phone and called not the police, but Monroe's personal psychoanalyst, Dr. Ralph Greenson.

The police were finally called and arrived on the scene the next morning. Later, Commander Jack Clemmons stated publicly, "In my opinion, Marilyn Monroe was murdered that night. In fact, it was the most obvious case of murder I ever saw. Everything was staged."

Monroe's body was placed on a gurney, covered, wheeled to the waiting ambulance, and transported to the Los Angeles County Coroner for an autopsy. Deputy Coroner Dr. Lionel Grandison performed the procedure and signed the death certificate, citing "acute barbiturate poisoning" as the cause of death. Later, he would reveal that he was forced to issue the cause of death under false pretenses, noting that some of the findings were purposefully disregarded.

And the little red diary given into evidence? It mysteriously disappeared.

Once the autopsy was completed, Monroe's body was transferred to Westwood Village Mortuary for preparation. Ex-husband Joe DiMaggio was on hand to handle the service arrangements. The funeral staff was given strict instructions that this was to be a private affair with no media. The guest list was limited to thirty-five people. Many of Monroe's friends and contemporaries were denied access to the funeral and felt slighted by the baseball star's lack of respect to the acting community.

At the service, Monroe was laid out in a green jersey dress with no other adornment inside her bronze casket with champagne velvet lining. DiMaggio placed a small bouquet of roses in her hands. Lee Strasburg performed the eulogy, describing the late actress as "a warm human being, impulsive, shy, sensitive, and in fear of rejection, yet ever avid for life and reaching out for fulfillment." Musical selections included "Over the Rainbow" and "Andante Cantabile" by Tchaikovsky.

At the end of the service, DiMaggio walked up to the casket and gently kissed Monroe before saying, "I love you, I love you." Her casket was then sealed and placed into the waiting hearse for the short ride to her final resting place in a small, secluded mausoleum. On each anniversary of her death, DiMaggio was known to place a red rose on her crypt until his death.

Many years later, in 1985, private investigator Fred Otash came forward in an interview with the *Los Angeles Times* and claimed that he had met with actor Peter Lawford the night of Marilyn's death. The allegation claimed that Lawford and Bobby Kennedy were both on the scene at Monroe's house that evening and Kennedy had escaped the city via helicopter.

JEAN HARLOW

The only accurate way to describe Jean Harlow is as "the gorgeous platinum blonde star who took Hollywood by storm." One would have never dreamed of the life awaiting this lovely young girl who grew up in the shadow of a controlling mother.

Harlow married at the age of sixteen and took off for the West Coast with her new husband in tow. Mama Jean followed closely behind with her good-for-nothing husband at her heels. Harlow's mother decided that her daughter was going to be a star — and that *she* would be the beneficiary of that fame and fortune.

Harlow began her career with bit parts upon her arrival in Hollywood, but soon Howard Hughes took notice of the striking blonde. He offered her a starring role in the film "Hell's Angels," and she was an instant success with audiences. Her sex appeal and sassy wit charmed men and women alike.

Writer Adele Rogers commented on Harlow, saying, "I found myself liking the girl. There was a directness, a simplicity, a hearty good humor and a joy of life about her that were irresistible."

Everyone who worked with Harlow took an immediate liking to her, including costar Clark Gable; they made a total of six films together. While filming "Goldie," costar Spencer Tracy advised Harlow to be herself and stop acting phony on the screen. She took his advice, and the two continued making pictures together to great success.

Harlow quickly kicked her useless husband to the curb shortly after her arrival in Hollywood. A single Harlow found a plethora of adoring men waiting to fill his shoes, but she did not find the next partner for her life until 1931, when she met MGM studio executive Paul Bern. Harlow enjoyed the stability and comfort. She was quoted as saying, "His friendship, his sane wisdom and his understanding were the great influences in my life."

The happy couple married July 2, 1932. After a glorious wedding and reception with many family and well-wishers, the newlyweds went back to Harlow's home for their wedding night. Early the next morning, Harlow called her friend Arthur Landau, asking him to come over and get her from their home. She later told Landau and his wife that Bern had a terrible secret that he had never revealed to her until their wedding night. His penis had not developed, and he was forced to use a phallus in order to make love to her. He begged Harlow to help him with his problem, saying, "You're a sex goddess. You can help me!" Harlow could do nothing to help the situation, and an irate Bern beat her until she was unconscious.

The couple stayed together for appearance's sake, but the love faded quickly, and rumors continued to spread that Bern beat Harlow on several occasions, causing her to have other health problems as a result. It was on September 4, 1932, that Harlow and Bern had yet another fight, sending Harlow to stay with her mother. Later that evening, Bern shot himself in the head, leaving a suicide note apologizing to Jean for their troubled marriage.

Despite the strain on her physically and emotionally, Harlow continued working. Her biggest hit came with the film, "Libeled Lady," opposite Spencer Tracy and William Powell in 1936. Powell and Harlow had been dating when he presented her with a $20,000-dollar engagement ring that Christmas. Harlow's life was like a dream — she had finally found the love she craved and the success achieved only by few of her contemporaries.

It was during the filming of her next film, "Saratoga," with Clark Gable that Harlow fell ill on the set, collapsing into her costar's arms. The studio heads wanted Harlow to seek medical attention, but Mama Jean insisted she would take care of her ailing daughter. Being a devout Christian Scientist, Mama Jean believed she could heal her daughter through the power of prayer and barricaded them in her home. Three days later, studio heads and friends forced their way in and found Harlow suffering and almost dead. They rushed her to the hospital, but by that time, it was too late. An inflamed gall bladder and kidney disease had left massive infection coursing through the young star's body. She received around-the-clock care, but this wasn't enough to save her.

Jean Harlow died June 7, 1937, at the age of twenty-six. The cause of death was uremic poisoning and cerebral edema. Rumors circulated later that the cause was poisoning from the bleach she used as a hair dye. Very few people, including close friends, knew that Harlow wore a wig for most of her career, her hair having been burned by the Clorox bleach she used to achieve the platinum effect. Another rumor was that she died of a botched abortion. None of these allegations were ever substantiated.

The funeral for Jean Harlow was a star-studded affair with more than 250 guests. Clark Gable, Spencer Tracy, Carole Lombard, Norma Shearer, Lionel Barrymore, and a host of others packed the small chapel at Forest Lawn in Glendale, California. Harlow lay in state with over $15,000 worth of flowers surrounding her casket. Fiancé William Powell purchased a private alcove for Harlow, and the front reads simply "Our Baby." Mama Jean made a reservation at the same location and later would join her daughter.

James Dean

Known to millions of adoring fans as "The Angry Young Man," James Dean touched audiences with his solemn, angry acting style. Though he performed in only three pictures during his short career, he will be forever remembered as the young, sexual creature woman adored.

Dean and his family moved to California in 1936 when he was just a young child. His mother died suddenly of uterine cancer, and his father shipped young Dean back to their hometown of Marion, Indiana, to live with his aunt and uncle.

After graduating from high school, Dean moved back to California to try to build a relationship with his estranged father and to get a degree from UCLA, but neither of these dreams came true. He dropped out of school, and he never achieved the closeness he craved from his only parent.

Dean moved to New York, was accepted into the elite Actors Studio, and began acting on Broadway, debuting in "The Jaguar" in 1952. By 1955, Dean was a moderate success on Broadway and was offered — and accepted — a role in the upcoming film "East of Eden." He was later nominated for an Academy Award for Best Actor. That same year, Dean would be cast in his most famous role, playing a young misfit teenager opposite the beautiful Natalie Wood in "Rebel Without a Cause."

Dean's next film, "Giant," costarring Elizabeth Taylor and Rock Hudson, would be his final screen appearance. The role won him a second Oscar nomination for Best Actor, announced posthumously.

Being a young man with great fame and wealth, Dean purchased a 1955 Porsche Spider and was looking forward to entering the car in road races in and around Los Angeles. On September 30, 1955, he and mechanic Rolf Wuetherich were heading to a road race in Salinas when he was pulled over for speeding. This was amusing to Dean since he had just two weeks earlier finished filming a public service announcement for the National Highway Committee encouraging safe driving. His final words into the camera were, "And remember, drive safely...because the life you save may be mine."

After the officer warned Dean to slow down, he took off again. Traveling the road at high speeds, he noticed another car coming toward them on the curving road. Dean commented to his passenger, "That guy's got to stop. He'll see us." With that comment, Dean crashed into the other car. His passenger was thrown from the vehicle and suffered a broken leg. The driver of the other car had only minor injuries. An ambulance arrived on the scene and transported the injured young man to a local hospital, but James Dean died of his injuries en route to the hospital. He was only twenty-four.

Dean's body was transported back to his hometown, where he was buried October 8, 1955. A memorial stone was constructed with a bust of the movie star on a pillar. This was stolen from the cemetery by an ardent fan and replaced at a later date.

Rumors, though, still circulate to this day that Dean did not actually die in the crash, but was badly disfigured and chose to disappear from public view.

CARL SWITZER

One of the lead actors in the "Little Rascals" was Carl Switzer, who played Alfalfa. Fate must have been shining on the young lad when he, brother Harold, and their mother were touring a movie studio while visiting family in 1934. Carl and his brother began performing in the public cafeteria as Hal Roach looked on during lunch. He hired both boys immediately, and Switzer, a self-proclaimed singer and musician, took to lead roles shortly after signing.

A precocious young man, Switzer loved a good prank, sometimes carrying things too far with his cast members. It is rumored that he caused severe injury to George "Spanky" MacFarland when he put fishhooks in his pants. Later in the series, he became destructive; urinating on the studio lights before filming began. Once the lights

The gravesite of Carl "Alfalfa" Switzer is located at Hollywood Forever Cemetery in Hollywood, California.

began to heat during the scene, a stench emanated from them, requiring filming to stop and costing valuable time. He was also known to have put chewing gum inside the camera, destroying the film and costing thousands to replace the equipment. Switzer's father offered no assistance, instead constantly arguing for higher pay and more screen time for his son.

The series ended at the end of 1940, and twelve-year-old Switzer tried in earnest to find work. He was offered a few minor roles in several films, including "Going My Way" and "It's A Wonderful Life" with Jimmy Stewart. In 1946, he was cast in the Gas House Kids series, a poor copy of "The Bowery Boys," reinventing his Alfalfa character. This series lasted only a year, leaving Switzer once again looking for work. He accepted a role in B westerns as a sidekick, but this was only temporary for the actor.

As an adult, Carl found more frustration in Hollywood and moved to Kansas to find work. Working on a farm in Pretty Prairie, he met Diane Collingwood, and the two married. Collingwood became pregnant not long after the marriage, but this did not prevent the couple from splitting four months later.

Continuing to look for work, Switzer decided to breed hunting dogs and become a hunting guide. He found little success, but was supported by not only his godparents Roy Rogers and Dale Evans, but also Jimmy Stewart.

In January 1959, Switzer borrowed a hunting dog from friend Moses "Bud" Stintz. The dog disappeared, and Switzer posted a $50-dollar reward for the dog's safe return. He received a call from a man claiming to have the dog, and the two set up a meeting at a local bar where Switzer was working part-time.

Not actually having the money to pay the reward, Switzer gave the man $35 in cash and $25 dollars worth of alcohol to settle the transaction. He returned the dog to Stintz, which should have been the end to the matter. Unfortunately, a few days later, on January 21, Switzer and a friend were discussing the matter while drinking and Switzer decided that Stintz owed *him* the $50 paid to find the dog. He went to Stintz's Mission Hills home to collect the money.

Arriving at the house, a drunken Switzer pounded on the front door. Stintz opened the door and Switzer entered, demanding his money. Facts surrounding what occurred varied according to those present, but according to accounts, an argument broke out and Switzer pulled a knife, threatening to kill Stintz. To defend himself, Stintz pulled a gun and shot Switzer in the groin as Switzer rushed him with the weapon.

Later, witness Tom Corrigan came forward, claiming that the physical altercation never occurred and that the knife in question was never used. Corrigan stated that Stintz came into the room brandishing the gun and shot Switzer before he had a chance to move, but Corrigan was never called to testify in the court proceedings. A Los Angeles judge closed the case, calling the killing a justifiable homicide and Stintz went free.

Carl Switzer's death went unnoticed by most of Hollywood; only a footnote in the newspaper followed the death. Headline news was claimed by the death of movie producer Cecil B. DeMille, who had passed away the same day.

Only family and friends attended a brief funeral. Switzer was buried in Hollywood Memorial Park in Los Angeles, California. His headstone depicts a Pete the Pup style of dog, which some say is a nod to his days in the Little Rascals series, but his family claimed it memorialized his career of breeding dogs.

HEATHER O'ROURKE

At the tender age of five, Heather Michele O'Rourke captured both America's heart and scared her audience silly, becoming a pop culture icon.

Born in San Diego, O'Rourke was only three years old when she won the Little Miss contest. With natural acting and dancing ability, she began modeling for Mattel Toys and appeared in commercials for the McDonalds fast-food restaurant chain.

One day, while O'Rourke was sitting in the commissary waiting for her mother, a stranger approached and asked her what her name was. "I am not allowed to talk to strangers," she replied. While the interchange was still going on, O'Rourke's mother appeared, and the man introduced himself as Steven Spielberg. He was looking for a six-year-old girl for his next picture and asked if O'Rourke could audition for the part.

The next day in Spielberg's office, O'Rourke laughed and acted just as a five-year-old child would. He felt she was too young, but asked her to come back the next day with a scary picture book. She arrived the next morning carrying the book. When Spielberg asked her to scream, she continued to scream until she broke down into tears. He told her mother after the interview was over, "I don't know what it is about her, but she's got the job."

The movie was a huge success at the box office with O'Rourke's famous line — "They're heeere!" — a high point in the movie. O'Rourke was offered a part on the series "Happy Days" and worked with the cast during the 1982 and 1983 seasons. She also brandished success with roles on "Fantasy Island," "Webster," and "Still the Beaver."

In 1985, O'Rourke was asked to reprise her role in the upcoming sequel, "Poltergeist II: The Other Side," changing her now-famous line to, "They're baaaack!" She was already slated to continue the series with "Poltergeist III" in 1988.

O'Rourke suffered from flu-like symptoms in January 1988 and was hospitalized briefly. Upon her release, the doctors medicated her, and she continued working on the film. Throughout filming, she never complained of any further problems and traveled with her family cross-country during a break in filming. It was on January 31, 1988, when O'Rourke appeared to worsen. She could not keep food in her stomach and, by the next morning, was unable to swallow food. Her mother quickly tried to dress her and take her to the hospital when the child collapsed. She was transported to Children's Hospital in San Diego, but suffered cardiac arrest en route. The doctors determined she had intestinal stenosis, which is more commonly known as a bowel obstruction, and immediately began operating on the young girl. O'Rourke died on the operating table of septic shock triggered by cardiopulmonary arrest at 2:40 p.m. on February 1, 1988.

Heather O'Rourke's funeral was private, attended by only family and few of her former co-stars at Westwood Memorial Park in Los Angeles. After the brief service, "Poltergeist" co-star Tom Skerritt acted as one of the pallbearers, carrying the small casket from the chapel at Westwood Memorial Park to her final resting place in the outdoor mausoleum next to writer Truman Capote. Her simple bronze marker reads "Carol Anne" — Poltergeist I, II, III. The filming of "Poltergeist III" finished with a body double, and her character was written out of the ending.

A 'Care Bear' teddy bear adorns the crypt of Heather O'Rourke at Pierce Brothers Westwood Memorial Park in Westwood, California.

JOHN CANDY

Considered one of the greatest funnymen of the 1970s and 1980s, John Candy started his career in East York, a suburb of Toronto, Canada. His father passed away from a heart attack when Candy was only five years old, an event Candy should have kept in mind later in his life.

Candy began acting with Toronto's Second City Troupe of Performers and appeared in SCTV in Toronto in the 1970s and 1980s. He had several offers from "Saturday Night Live" producer Lorne Michaels, but refused, choosing instead to stay loyal to his troupe from Canada. Candy appeared in many Canadian television and film productions, including "It Seemed Like a Good Idea," "Find the Lady," and "The Silent Partner."

Moving to Hollywood, Candy established himself with his unusual humor and uncanny imitations, which won him small roles in the 1979 hit "1941," "The Blues Brothers" in 1980, and "Stripes" in 1981. One critic described Candy's performance as "the big blob farmer from Second City."

Continuing to win these minor roles throughout the early 1980s, Candy would become part of the supporting cast of such classic films as "National Lampoon's Vacation," "Splash," and "Little Shop of Horrors." He turned down the role of Louis Tully in the 1984 blockbuster film "Ghostbusters."

In the mid-1980s, Candy continued acting, but the scripts he chose for himself were poor, causing his success to wane. Movies like "Armed and Dangerous," "Summer Rental," and "Who's Harry Crumb?" were not big box-office successes for Candy, who continued partaking in the same fat funnyman role, pigeonholing himself and his acting skills. One breakout hit for him would be opposite Steve Martin in "Planes, Trains and Automobiles," playing salesman Del Griffith, his most critically acclaimed role.

Wanting to break into dramatic roles, Candy would accept a cameo role in "Home Alone" and then star opposite veteran actress Catherine O'Hara in "Only the Lonely." Candy would have another huge success with the film "Cool Running," based on the true story of the Jamaican bobsled team's debut at the 1988 Olympics.

Candy accepted a starring role in the film "Wagons East" in the summer of 1994 and traveled to Mexico for filming. He predicted to Catherine O'Hara "something bad is going to happen there," but chose to honor his commitment. Candy had been warned by his physician that he needed to lose some of the three hundred pounds of weight he carried on his frame his entire life, but Candy felt this would jeopardize his funnyman status.

John Candy died of a fatal heart attack in Durango, Mexico, March 4, 1994. A funeral was held March 9 in Los Angeles, California, and was broadcast live on Canadian television. Fellow funnymen Chevy Chase, Bill Murray, Martin Short, Rick Moranis, and Dan Aykroyd attended, along with a host of other stars, with Aykroyd giving the eulogy. He was laid to rest in the mausoleum at Holy Cross Catholic Cemetery in Culver City, California, in a crypt above famed actor Fred MacMurray.

Candy will be forever remembered as a brilliant comedian and a truly gifted performer.

Crypt of John Candy at Holy Cross Memorial Park in Culver City, California.

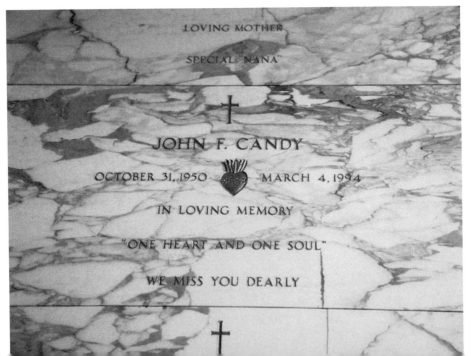

River Phoenix

The blonde-haired, blue-eyed teen was considered one of the most talented young people in Hollywood during the last part of the 1980s. River Phoenix's tragic end outside a nightclub in Hollywood continues to rock the entertainment industry to this day.

Born on a farm in Oregon, River Phoenix was the first child of John and Arlyn Bottom, both flower children of the 1960s. By the time he was two years old, his parents had joined and begun traveling with the radical cult group Children of God. The family kept on the move, traveling to Texas, Mexico, Puerto Rico, and South America. Phoenix's mother gave birth to a girl, Rain Bottom, and the two children would sing on the streets for money to help the family survive.

In 1978, the Bottom family left the group and traveled by steamer back to the United States, where they settled in Florida. A third child arrived, Summer Joy, and by then the parents had opted to change their last name to Phoenix.

The Phoenix children continued to support their parents by singing in the streets and in local talent contests. Phoenix's mother decided to move her children to Hollywood, with dreams of stardom for her family. She set out on a quest to make sure her children would become famous so "they could make the world a better place." She got a job as a secretary for NBC Studios and pushed her eldest child in front of notable agent Iris Burton, who took to him instantly, sensing a star quality about the child.

Burton started them out doing commercials, but Phoenix felt they were too phony and opted not to continue. He was given several small parts on children's television programs and also appeared in the 1982 series "Seven Brides for Seven Brothers," which was short-lived.

Phoenix moved into small dramatic parts in made-for-television movies and appeared in his first major motion picture "Explorers" in 1985 opposite newcomer Ethan Hawke.

In the summer of 1986, Phoenix and three hundred other hopefuls auditioned for a part in the Rob Reiner film "Stand By

Me." Reiner's calm directing and Phoenix's friendships with the other young actors on the set helped to advance his acting ability. It was on the set of that film that Phoenix would have his first experience with cigarettes, alcohol, and marijuana.

In Phoenix's next film "The Mosquito Coast," director Peter Weir would later comment about the young talent that there was "something apart from the acting ability." He was considered an old soul in the face of a vulnerable child.

Phoenix's next performance, in the film "Running on Empty," garnered him an Academy Award nomination for Best Actor in a Supporting Role. Phoenix was truly a star and was respected by those who worked with him, but his father was concerned about the influence of the entertainment industry on a young man and purchased a large ranch in Florida for his family. Unfortunately, it was too late to save his son from the lifestyle he had learned in California. Phoenix formed a band called Aleka's Attic and started drinking heavily and using cocaine. He continued to blossom as an actor, but those around him were noticing a change.

Phoenix's demeanor was turning dark and his body becoming pale and thin. The positive disposition had turned cynical and edgy. During shooting of his next movie, "The Thing Called Love," Phoenix was often under the influence of a controlled substance. He attempted to clean up his act during the filming of "Dark Blood" in 1993, but during a break, he was ready to party and went looking for a good time.

On the evening of October 30, 1993, Phoenix, girlfriend Samantha Mathis, younger brother Joaquin, and sister Rain were at the Hotel Nikkon drinking heavily. In the later hours of the night, they went to the Viper Room on Sunset Boulevard, owned by friend Johnny Depp, who was playing that night with famed rock band The Red Hot Chili Peppers. Phoenix was already inebriated and had done several drugs that night. He entered the bathroom at the club and was offered a hit of an exotic form of heroin. His body immediately began rejecting the drug, causing him to vomit and shake uncontrollably. Another patron gave him a hit of Valium to relax him. He lost consciousness for a short time and then told his friends he needed a breath of fresh air. Assisted by his brother, Phoenix was carried out of the club. He commented to the doorman before leaving, "I'm gonna die, dude."

Once outside, Phoenix collapsed on the sidewalk and went into convulsions, his head hitting the sidewalk violently and his arms and legs flailing. Joaquin called 911 and yelled into the phone, "You must get here, please, he's dying!" Meanwhile, Rain knelt down and attempted to hold her brother's head still while they waited for the ambulance.

A crowd gathered around the scared group until the emergency team arrived less than five minutes later. Phoenix had gone into cardiac arrest, and the team worked to revive him en route to Cedars-Sinai Medical Center. Doctors worked quickly to install a pacemaker, but their efforts were in vain. The young, talented star was pronounced dead at 1:51 a.m. on October 31, 1993. The cause of death: acute multiple drug intoxication.

The next day, floral tributes and spray-painted graffiti littered the front of the Viper Room in remembrance of the fallen celebrity. The club would remain closed for the next ten days in tribute to Johnny Depp's friend.

True to form, River Phoenix's parents made a statement from their home in Gainesville, Florida: "His beauty, gentleness, compassion, vulnerability, and love are gifts for all eternity." They asked that the public make contributions to Phoenix's favorite charities in lieu of flowers. There would be no public funeral service, his parents instead to cremate Phoenix's body and scatter his ashes over the ranch in Florida.

Unfortunately, this would not be the end of the story for this tragic actor who was loved by those who knew him. Soon after his death, the insurance company that backed the film "Dark Blood" sued the estate for $6 million dollars, the amount paid by backers of the unfinished film. The claim was that Phoenix had not disclosed his drug problem as per his contract. Fortunately for the family, Phoenix had never signed the form, and the case was thrown out of court.

River Phoenix was also slated for the role of the interviewer in "Interview with a Vampire." The role would be played by his friend, actor Christian Slater, who donated his salary from the film to Phoenix's favorite charity.

Some years before his death, Phoenix was quoted as saying, "I would rather quit while I was ahead. No need in overstaying your welcome."

JOHN RITTER

John Ritter seemed almost destined for a career in the entertainment industry. Son to the country and western singer Tex Ritter and actress Dorothy Faye, Ritter would follow in his parents' footsteps, making his own mark on the world of film and television.

Born in Burbank, California, Ritter attended school in Los Angeles and graduated from famed Hollywood High School, where he excelled, being voted both class president and class clown during his tenure. His father went abroad to entertain the troops, and son John followed his dad to Germany, performing in a series of plays during this time.

Seriously thinking of a career in politics, Ritter's parents had him all set to continue his education and become a lawyer. Instead, Ritter enrolled at the University of Southern California and majored in psychology and minored in architecture. After a couple of years, he changed his major to theater arts and studied drama with famed acting coach Stella Adler. He graduated in 1971 with a Bachelor in Fine Arts for drama.

Upon graduating, Ritter started acting, doing bit parts in film and television. His face could be seen in a number of hit television shows during the 1970s. He had walk-on roles in shows like "Dan August," "Medical Center," "MASH," "Kojak," and "The Bob Newhart Show." He would find his first steady role in the drama "The Waltons" as Reverend Mathew Fordwick, appearing in eighteen episodes from 1972 through 1976. Also in 1976, Ritter appeared on the popular game show "The Dating Game," winning a vacation to Lake Havasu.

In 1977, Ritter auditioned for the lead in a new situation comedy, "Three's Company," based on the popular British series "Man About the House." He was cast for the role, beating out fifty other actors vying for it (including newcomer Billy Crystal). To round out the cast, Joyce DeWitt and pretty blonde Suzanne Somers were cast as the roommates, and the series debuted as a summer replacement show.

Gravesite of John Ritter at Forest Lawn Memorial Park in Hollywood Hills, California.

Audiences were attracted to the show, enjoying the slapstick comedy of Ritter. He received an Emmy, Golden Globe, and People's Choice award for his role of Jack Tripper. He would continue with the series from 1977 through 1984, receiving critical acclaim for his comedic timing and sharp wit.

In the final seasons of the show, the producers were having difficulty with Ritter's costars and the show was not picked up for the 1985 season. A spin-off, "Three's A Crowd," starred Ritter as the same character who had moved in with his girlfriend with a meddling father. The show was short-lived, and Ritter moved on to "Hooperman" and "Fish Police," both shows lasting only one season.

In 1992, Ritter found moderate success with the show "Hearts Afire," which ran from 1992 through 1995. He would also continue acting on the big screen with parts in small films like "Skin Deep" and "Stay Tuned." He would find greater success with a surprise hit "Problem Child" in 1990 and returned for the sequel, "Problem Child 2," in 1991.

Ritter, aching to move into more dramatic roles, took a part in Billy Bob Thorton's "Slingblade," playing a homosexual. He also continued acting on the stage, appearing in over fifty productions on Broadway, including Neil Simon's "The Dinner Party."

In 2002, Ritter was cast as the father in the new comedy "8 Simple Rules for Dating My Teenage Daughter," playing opposite seasoned veteran actress Katey Sagal. The show addressed many of the topics of this new generation: sex, drugs, and dealing with being arrested were welcome storylines for the cast. The show was an instant success, winning Best New Comedy at the People's Choice Awards that year.

Riding high on the huge success of the hit show, Ritter attended the ABC Primetime Preview Weekend at Disney's California Adventure at the beginning of September 2003. He signed autographs and posed for pictures with hundreds of adoring fans in the blistering Southern California heat, showing everyone he met unending attention.

On September 11, 2003, Ritter arrived on the set and spoke with long-time friend Henry Winkler, who was making a guest appearance on the show that week. He confessed to Winkler that he felt ill and had severe chest pains. The cast rushed him across the road to Providence St. Joseph Medical Center of Burbank, the same hospital he had been born in fifty-four years earlier. Ritter became quite sick and his condition deteriorated quickly. Doctors diagnosed Ritter with aorta dissection, a rare heart disease leading to catastrophic failure of the aorta, and rushed him into surgery, but they were too late to save the actor. John Ritter died on the operating table at 10 p.m., just six days before his fifty-fifth birthday.

A private funeral was held on September 15, 2003, at the Forest Lawn Memorial Park in Hollywood Hills, and he was laid to rest in the same area as comedy legends Buster Keaton, Marty Feldman, and Stan Laurel.

Michael Jackson

Michael Jackson's star on the Hollywood Walk of Fame was adorned with fan memorabilia after his death.

Of the singing acts to emerge from the 1970s, one group's meteoric rise was due largely to the youngest child and front man Michael Jackson. The Jackson family, led by father Joe, took the music industry by storm and the pint-size Michael radiated charm, talent, and pop star looks. The Jackson 5 toured the country and gained huge national success with their television appearances. By 1969, the five brothers were producing back-to-back hits.

While continuing his success with the family act, Jackson took the role of the scarecrow in the 1977 production of "The Wiz" with

Diana Ross. His performance showcased his dancing ability and solo voice to the world. Quincy Jones was on hand to write the score for the movie, and an introduction to Jackson was arranged.

Jones produced Jackson's first solo album Off the Wall, and Jackson found huge success with several chart-topping singles. The driving beat and memorable lyrics resonated with audiences, soaring Jackson's career to new heights. The world had only begun its love affair with this talented young man who already had a lifetime of success behind him.

Jackson's second album, Thriller, released in 1982, took the world by storm, producing seven hit singles for the pop star and becoming the top-selling album in history, with over fifty million copies sold. Songs like "Billie Jean," "Pretty Young Thing," and the title cut "Thriller" found their way to the top of the charts, into dance clubs, and on television.

With the birth of MTV and the music video, Jackson found a golden opportunity to showcase his music and talent on the small screen. The epic fourteen-minute "Thriller" became a bestselling home video; it included footage of rehearsals and a look at Jackson's private life.

Jackson, winning an unprecedented eight, swept the 1984 Grammy Awards. That same year, he officially broke off from the Jackson 5 to continue a solo career. His second album Bad, while not quite the success of Thriller, continued to show the versatility of the singer with another string of hits. Jackson's world tour that followed became one of the greatest success stories in music history, and, by the end of the 1980s, Jackson had been named artist of the decade.

With scores of fans and admirers worldwide, rumors began to circulate about what some considered bizarre behavior in the superstar. Jackson's home was dubbed Neverland Ranch; he installed several carnival rides on the property and purchased many exotic animals, including a chimp he named Bubbles. Jackson invited children onto the property and spent large amounts of time with the young actor Macaulay Culkin, star of the popular "Home Alone" movies.

The Hall of Liberty where the private Jackson family memorial was held at Forest Lawn Memorial Park in Hollywood Hills, California.

In 1993, Jackson was accused of sexually abusing a minor who had visited his home. The young boy made claims that the pop star had touched him and described his genitalia in detail to police investigators. Jackson publicly announced his innocence to the world, but the suit was settled out of court for an undisclosed amount of money, furthering speculation on Jackson's lifestyle.

It was during this time Jackson became involved with long-time acquaintance Lisa Marie Presley, and the two married. The couple made several public appearances together, holding hands and kissing for the cameras. While publicly showing genuine affection, the couple divorced less than two years later.

Jackson continued with what people considered erratic behavior. He had several plastic surgeries that dramatically changed his appearance and the tabloids accused the singer of sleeping in a glass chamber, bleaching his skin, and a variety of other odd behaviors.

Jackson surprised fans when he announced a second marriage and later became a father, naming his first son Prince. In the years that followed, Jackson fathered two more children, but questions about his state of mind arose when he appeared in public with veils over his and the children's faces and dangled his infant son Blanket over the balcony of his hotel for fans below.

In 2003, Jackson found himself in the eye of another storm, being accused once again of child abuse. Among the seven counts was the accusation of plying the child with alcohol to commit the crime. The five-month trial began in Santa Maria, California, with Jackson showing up frail and thin. Fans continued to support him, showing up at the courthouse with signs and cheering at his arrival. Jackson was acquitted of all charges, but the damage to his image had been done. Jackson moved out of the country, fleeing the media that had plagued him for so many years.

It was in 2008 that Jackson announced he would be making a comeback with a fifty-date series of performances in London, followed by an album and new videos. The public waited expectantly for the concert dates, selling out all performances. His career and personal life seemed to be on the rise as he made preparations for the coming year.

In June 2009, Jackson arrived in Los Angeles to work with choreographers on the production. It was June 25, 2009, that Jackson was in a rented home in Los Angeles when he collapsed and stopped breathing. Paramedics were called and arrived within ten minutes of the call. Jackson's personal physician had been trying to resuscitate the icon and the medical personnel continued CPR en route to the hospital. Upon his arrival at UCLA Medical Center in Westwood, doctors continued working to revive him, but were unsuccessful. Michael Jackson was pronounced dead at 2:26 p.m. at the age of fifty.

The media and many concerned fans had converged on the hospital, waiting for an update. A press conference that afternoon confirmed that the self-proclaimed King of Pop was dead. Fans around the world were devastated upon hearing the news and almost immediately, tributes to Jackson appeared at his star on the Hollywood Walk of Fame, his family home in Encino, California, and the Neverland Ranch in Santa Barbara, California. Thousands of floral tributes, cards, and letters, pouring out the admiration and love from thousands of people young and old, lay on the ground just outside the gates of his home.

The days that followed his death were filled with extensive media coverage. The world sat by the television, waiting to hear the latest news of the singer's final moments. Funeral plans were announced and then changed several times, frustrating those who wanted to make plans to travel to California for the memorial. Finally, the Jackson family announced a grand memorial tribute at the Staples Center in downtown Los Angeles to be held July 7, 2009. A lottery for tickets to the memorial found people scrambling to obtain entry to the most sought-after event in music history. Fans flew to Los Angeles from all over the world in hopes that their names would be one of the lucky few to be awarded the prized tickets.

The morning of July 7, 2009, the Jackson family held a private tribute for their beloved son, brother, and father with just the family present at Forest Lawn Memorial Park in Los Angeles, California. Twenty black vehicles ranging from Rolls Royce's to Range Rover SUVs entered through the cemetery gates and followed in procession to Freedom Court, where the funeral for the singing star was held. After the brief service, the gold casket with a spray of red flowers was loaded into the hearse and, with the body of Michael Jackson leading the way, the procession continued to the Staples Center for the public memorial.

The Los Angeles police got a pleasant surprise from fans. Those in attendance were orderly and respectful of the downtown area, creating a pleasant atmosphere. Only 1,000 onlookers arrived on the scene and remained behind barricades. Inside the venue, a quiet reverence descended on the crowd as pallbearers transported the gold casket carrying Jackson's body to a raised area below the stage. The star-studded event included performances by Mariah Carey, Usher, Jennifer Hudson, and Jermaine Jackson. Queen Latifah read a poem by renowned poet Maya Angelou and eulogies were read by the Reverend Al Sharpton, actress Brooke Shields, and sports superstar Magic Johnson, giving the audience a look into the private life of the pop star.

The end of the service brought the performers together to sing the 1984 hit song "We Are the World," with the entire Jackson family coming on stage to blend their voices. At the end of the service, Jackson's daughter Paris gave her own heartfelt goodbye to her father. The entire world was privileged to witness the pure love of the little girl as she stated: "Ever since I was born, Daddy has been the best father you could ever imagine. I just want to say I love him so much." The child then broke down and was escorted off the stage by her aunt, Janet Jackson.

The question on everyone's lips was where the body of Michael Jackson would ultimately rest. Rumors began early, saying the family would have Jackson interred at his beloved Neverland Ranch, but the county of Santa Barbara would not give permission. Finally, on September 4, 2009, a private funeral was held — and Michael Jackson was at last laid to rest — at Forest Lawn Memorial Park with longtime pals Macaulay Culkin and screen legend Elizabeth Taylor in attendance.

However, the saga of Jackson's death doesn't end there. As of this writing, the criminal investigation of his final days was continuing, as the police were investigating the role Jackson's personal physician had in his fatal overdose.

Chapter Four:

FAREWELL TO OUR MOST BELOVED STARS

The lives of Hollywood's greatest stars have always been embraced by their adoring fans, but the deaths of these stars have become even more fascinating. The life lived becomes even more dear to us when their final moments are a treasury of the happiness brought to others throughout their lives. Here are just a few of the endearing ends of Hollywood's most beloved stars.

LOU COSTELLO

Lou Costello is best known for his comedy antics with Bud Abbott in the Abbott and Costello movies and television shows. Costello began his career working as a carpenter for the movie studios while doing comedy in Vaudeville. He became a stunt man before moving to New York. One evening, when the straight man for Budd Abbott took ill, Costello offered to fill in for him, and a comedy duo was born.

The crypt of Lou Costello bears his legal name at Calvary Cemetery in Los Angeles.

The two toured throughout the 1930s with the Vaudeville circuit and finally landed a part on the Kate Smith Radio Hour. This would give them national attention, and they soon signed a contract with Universal Pictures. They were given a small part in their first motion picture "One Night in the Tropics" and stole every scene with their antics. The studio decided to feature the team in "Buck Privates," with the popular singing group The Andrews Sisters. Throughout the 1940s, these two comedy geniuses were a major commodity for the studio, appearing in dozens of films during this time.

Costello and his wife, Anne, married in 1934, and and had three children together. The couple was devastated in 1943, when Lou Jr. wandered into the backyard, fell into the family's swimming pool, and drowned just before his first birthday. Though he never said so publicly, Costello blamed his wife for the death, feeling she should have been watching him more closely.

Costello's wife would turn to alcohol to drown her guilt and grief, and Costello would create the Lou Costello Jr. Youth Foundation, a recreational building erected for the city of Los Angeles youth programs. Privately, he would turn to gambling and food to ease his suffering, but he never really got over the death of his young son.

Costello turned his focus on his career and continued to see his popularity soar with the comedy act he created with partner Bud Abbott. The comedy team would have great success with "The Abbott and Costello Show" in the late 1940s until the outbreak of World War II.

With their popularity fading, the two stars found themselves performing in monster movies like "Abbot and Costello Meet Frankenstein" in 1948. Audiences were delighted with their antics and the movies were a huge box office success.

Costello struggled with his partner's ever-increasing drinking habit. He severed the relationship after Abbott showed up drunk for a performance in front of the NBC executives. The sudden breakup of the masters of comedy brought to an end a great era. After the breakup, Abbott sued Costello for over $200,000; he claimed that this was the amount he had earned during the run of their television show, but never received.

On February 26, 1959, Costello suffered a heart attack and was taken to Doctor's Hospital in Beverly Hills. In the days that followed, his health continued to suffer, and he succumbed to a second attack while hospitalized. Family and friends gathered around him, waiting for the final moments when the beloved actor would be taken from them.

On March 3, 1959, Costello felt much better and chatted with his manager, Eddie Sherman. During the conversation, Costello asked Sherman to go out and buy him a strawberry ice cream soda. He had missed some of life's little pleasures and wanted a taste of the world outside of the hospital food he was being fed daily. Sherman honored his wish and returned shortly with the soda hidden so as not to alert the hospital staff.

Costello and Sherman chatted about the future while Costello enjoyed his ice cream soda. After he finished, he remarked, "That's the best ice cream soda I ever tasted." Immediately after uttering these words, Costello suffered another massive heart attack and the world lost another comedy icon. We should all be so lucky to have one last taste of our favorite things in this life just before leaving it.

Costello's funeral was attended by fellow funnymen Red Skelton, Danny Thomas, and Joe E. Brown, among others. A visibly emotional Bud Abbott led the pallbearers carrying the casket to its final resting place at Calvary Cemetery in Los Angeles, California. Lou was placed in the same mausoleum as his infant son. The name on his crypt reads "Lou Francis Cristillo" Costello's birth name.

GEORGE BURNS & GRACIE ALLEN

George Burns and Gracie Allen were undoubtedly one of the most successful comedy teams ever. On the radio and television, Allen played the dim-witted wife. Burns was reported as saying, "She was the smartest dumbbell in the history of show business."

Their affection for each other was obvious in both their performances and their private life. They married in 1926 and never left each other's side until 1958, when Allen suffered a heart condition and was forced to leave show business. She led a quiet life until August 27, 1964, when she suffered a massive heart attack and passed away with Burns at her side.

After her death, Allen was buried at Forest Lawn Memorial Park in Glendale, California. Burns would visit her monthly, sitting on the bench in front of the white marble crypt in the quiet mausoleum. He

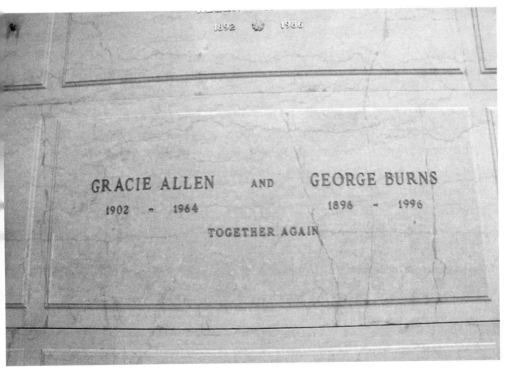

Crypt of George Burns and Gracie Allen at the Freedom Mausoleum in Forest Lawn Memorial Park, Glendale, California.

would catch her up on the latest news and continue to let her know of his love for her. He was quoted as saying, "I tell her everything that's going on. I don't know if she hears me, but I do know that every time I talk to her, I feel better."

Burns continued to work steadily and remained healthy until 1994, when he was injured in his bathtub in his Beverly Hills home. On January 20, 1996, he celebrated his 100th birthday, but was unable to attend the party due to his failing health. Two months later, he was sitting in bed, looking at photographs of him and Allen over the years. Rumors state that he looked at his nurse and said, "I hope Gracie looks young and beautiful when we meet again...and I hope I'm not stuck looking like the one-hundred-year-old man I've become since she left."

On March 9, 1996, George Burns passed away quietly at his home. Irving Fein, his great friend and manager, stated afterward, "There was no pain or suffering. After George drew in his last breath, he had a smile on his face."

For his memorial service, Burns was dressed by his long-time valet in a light blue shirt, blue tie, and one of his favorite suits. He had cash in his pocket (no one knows the exact amount, but it has been said it was anywhere from $300 to $1,000), a deck of cards (in case a bridge game came up), three cigars, and his keys. The small funeral, attended by friends and family, was held at the Wee Kirk of the Heather Chapel at Forest Lawn Memorial Park. He was interred in the same crypt as his beloved wife. He had one last request before his passing: "Make sure Gracie gets top billing." If you visit the site, you'll note that Allen's name is above Burns' on the crypt.

Several years before he died, Burns had stated that he was looking forward to death, knowing he would be with Allen again in Heaven.

WILLIAM RANDOLPH HEARST & MARION DAVIES

The longtime love affair between William Randolph Hearst and Marion Davies was well-known throughout early Hollywood, but began with speculation that Davies was a gold-digger vying for a "Sugar Daddy." What came to be was a romance of epic proportion, bridging time, age, and hardship.

Hearst, a well-known public figure, was the son of a wealthy silver-mining family and publisher of several newspapers, allowing his lavish lifestyle with his wife, Millicent Wilson. The two had four sons together, but affections became strained over the years.

Hearst became enamored with young starlet Marion Davies and decided she needed to become a movie star. He developed

Private Family Mausoleum of William Randolph Hearst in Colma, California.

Cosmopolitan Pictures specifically to further her career. He insisted that Davies play in serious movies only, uninterested in her natural ability for comedy. His determination to further her career actually backfired, causing strain between the young actress and the studio executives.

The couple lived together openly in Santa Monica, California, where Hearst built a lovely home for his mistress. The couple's lavish Hollywood parties were among the most sought after invitations by the motion picture elite.

A jealous man, Hearst would have Davies followed by private investigators, contantly believing she was having an affair behind his back. It was in 1924 that he was convinced she and movie star Charlie Chaplin had become lovers. It is alleged that the group set sail on Hearst's yacht along with several other guests. Hearst, determined to catch the two dallying, allegedly shot producer Tom Ince, and a huge cover-up ensued. History would prove later that the incident was greatly overblown.

Hearst very much wanted to marry Davies, but his wife's divorce terms were too high. He opted instead to stay married and simply continue his relationship with Davies. The two remained ever faithful to each other and Davies even sold several of her possessions to give Hearst $1 million dollars after the Stock Market crash in 1929.

In the 1930s, Davies retired from motion pictures to devote herself full-time to the ailing Hearst. She stayed by his side, watching his health decline until 1951. It was on the night of August 14, 1951, that William Randolph Hearst lay on his deathbed with the ever-present Davies by his side. Several doctors and Hearst's attorney tried in vain to convince Davies to get some rest. The attorney finally slipped a sedative into a drink given to the actress. While Davies slept, Hearst died peacefully at the age of eighty-eight.

When Davies awoke, she found Hearst was gone, the room cleared of all his belongings as if he had never been there at all. She was beside herself, having never had the opportunity to say goodbye to her lifelong companion.

Millicent Hearst scheduled a grand funeral for her husband. Hearst's body was taken to Pierce Brothers Mortuary in Los Angeles

Private Family Mausoleum of Marion Davies with her given name at Hollywood Forever Memorial Park.

and prepared for transportation back to San Francisco. Hearst's four sons were on hand to oversee preparations. As the body was flown to Northern California, a slight detour was made to fly over Hearst Castle, where the pilot tipped the plane's wing in tribute.

For two days, Hearst's body lay in state at Grace Episcopal Church on Nob Hill, laid out in a dark blue suit, blue tie, and monogrammed shirt in a bronze casket. Thousands passed by to pay their final respects, as 1,500 friends and family attended the formal ceremony. Hearst's wife ensured that Marion Davies would not attend the event, telling her sons, "He's mine now. He's finally mine."

Hundreds of flower arrangements from those who had done business with the business magnate banked the walls of the church.

The ceremony was presided over by the Reverend Karl M. Block, Episcopal Bishop of California. The church was filled with the music of Cesar Franck and Bach. A full choir closed the service with the 23rd Psalm.

The procession that followed the service included two-dozen limousines following the road to Cypress Lawn Cemetery outside San Francisco, California. William Randolph Hearst was laid to rest in a grand private family mausoleum with his parents. While the funeral was everything the family wished for to honor a great man, his true love, Davies, was not welcome to say her final goodbyes to her great love.

Life After Hearst

Ten weeks after the passing of Hearst, Marion Davies married Horace Brown, but the marriage was not a happy one. Marion filed for divorce twice, but neither was ever finalized.

Marion led a quiet life in her later years, contributing over $1 million dollars to the UCLA Children's Clinic that still bears her name today. Marion suffered a stroke in 1956 and was diagnosed with cancer of the jaw. Not long after, she fell and broke her leg causing more pain and suffering. The last appearance she made was in 1960 on "Hedda Hoppa's Hollywood."

Marion Davies died of cancer September 22, 1961. Her funeral at Immaculate Heart of Mary Church in Los Angeles, California, was attended by the Hollywood elite, including Mary Pickford, Clark Gable, and President Herbert Hoover. She was laid to rest in a private family mausoleum near the lake at Hollywood Memorial Park in Los Angeles, California.

Long after the death of Marion Davies, a woman named Patricia Van Cleve came forward on her deathbed and told her son that she was actually the daughter of Marion and William Randolph Hearst. Patricia had been raised as Marion's niece and was sworn to secrecy about the birth. After Patricia's death, it was proven that she was in fact the love child of Marion and William and she was laid to rest at the foot of her mother's mausoleum.

WALT DISNEY

Considered the most influential, powerful moviemaker in Hollywood history, Walter Elias Disney could never have known the impact he would have on the motion picture industry and the world during his 43-year career creating some of the best-loved animated classics the world has ever known. His theme parks and modern innovations to film and television made Walt Disney a true legend all over the world.

Even as a child, Disney was industrious, having two paper routes and working in a candy store during school recess. Unable to join the military at the age of sixteen, Disney joined the Red Cross and drove an ambulance. The ambulance he drove was always distinguishable due to the cartoons covering most of its exposed surface.

After he returned from his tour of duty, Disney went back to Kansas and worked for an advertising company while continuing his

Private Family garden of Walt Disney at Forest Lawn Memorial Park Glendale, California.

own work. By 1920, he had created his own cartoons and developed new processes to combine the animation with live action.

In August 1923, Disney moved to California with $40 in his pocket, his drawing materials, and a dream to make his own animated movies. By 1928, he had created the character Mortimer Mouse, which would later become the world-renowned Mickey Mouse. His first full-length cartoon starred Mickey in "Plane Crazy" along with girlfriend Minnie Mouse. Prior to the release, Disney created another featurette, "Steamboat Willie," and this sound picture would be the first one released to the public on November 18, 1928.

Disney continued his success and won the first of his thirty-two Academy Awards with the film "Flowers and Trees" in 1937. That same year, he stretched the bounds of imagination with the full-length feature animated classic "Snow White and the Seven Dwarves," the first film of its kind. Over the next decade, he would create many more beloved features, including "Cinderella," "Dumbo," "Fantasia," and "Bambi." The studio thrived in the years following the Great Depression, allowing Disney to expand production and hire over 1,000 artists to produce these films.

It was in 1954 when Disney was taking his daughter to ride the carousel that he realized there needed to be some form of entertainment that could include the entire family. He purchased an orange grove in Anaheim, California, and began the Herculean task of converting this rough land into a wonderland for all ages. In the span of one year, his dream came true, and Disneyland opened July 17, 1955. Speculation grew as to whether or not the park would be a success, some betting on the ultimate failure of the operation within a few years. Within thirty days, one million people had entered the gates of Disneyland, showing doubters that this investment was a huge success.

In the 1950s and 1960s, Disney took advantage of the newest medium — television — to give home viewers a look at the theme park and creating adventures in wildlife never before seen. He was a visionary, using television to advertise his projects and create excitement before they were even completed.

With the success of his first theme park, Disney decided to once again reach for the stars and purchased forty-three square miles of land in central Florida to create his next vision. Walt Disney World opened October 1, 1971, but its creator would not be there to see the reality of his dream.

In 1966, Disney was scheduled for surgery on an old neck injury. On November 2, the doctors took x-rays and found a large tumor on his left lung. When they performed the surgery to remove the cancer, the doctors were unable to save any part of the lung and were forced to remove it entirely. After chemotherapy, Disney and his wife retired to their home in Palm Springs during his recovery and returned to Los Angeles shortly after. It was on November 30, 1966, that Disney collapsed and was taken to the hospital. Unfortunately, he would not be released again to continue his legacy. Walt Disney died December 15, 1966, just ten days after his sixty-fifth birthday.

The only request Disney made prior to his death was that there would be a private funeral and burial with only family present. The family complied, having Disney's body cremated and buried in a small family plot at Forest Lawn Memorial Park in Glendale, California. It was only after the funeral and burial were complete that the family announced publicly that Walt Disney had died. When there was no public memorial for the great man, rumors began to circulate that Disney had been cryogenically frozen and stored beneath the Pirates of the Caribbean ride at Disneyland until a cure could be found for his cancer.

Even in death, Walt Disney continues to touch the lives of people of all ages. During his lifetime, he produced eighty-one feature films, theme parks, and technical innovations that will never be forgotten.

Chapter Five:

Stars' Tragic Endings

With the fantasy of Tinseltown, often we think the lives of the celebrities we see on the screen mimic the glamour we see in the darkened theater. They make us laugh and cry, giving the audience their all, yet never allowing the fans to realize the painful existence they sometimes lead. As a result, the tragic endings to some of the most beloved movie stars of our time creates a new facet, revealing the truth behind the camera.

JUDY GARLAND

Born Frances Ethel Gumm in Grand Rapids, Minnesota, Judy Garland was the youngest child of Frank Gumm, a Vaudeville Irish tenor, and Ethel Marion, a movie-house piano player.

When Garland was just two years old, her father managed a movie house where mama played during the silent films. Garland and her sisters entertained on the stage at intermission and, at Christmastime, the toddler was a smash hit with theatergoers, singing "Jingle Bells" while the audience soaked up her childlike charms. She had to be dragged, kicking and screaming, off the stage that night by her grandmother, but her mother was already hatching a plan for her littlest daughter.

With a struggling marriage, Ethel Gumm decided she would put all of her energies into making her daughters famous. She took full control of the family, moving them to Lancaster, California, seventy miles north of Los Angeles. She enrolled her girls in the Meglin Kiddies talent school, making sure they excelled at singing and dancing.

In 1933, Mama Gumm would take her daughters' act on the road to the World's Fair in Chicago, where she changed their last name to Garland. Her youngest she renamed "Judy Garland."

After many failed auditions for the major movie studios, Garland was called to MGM for an audition with Roger Edens. She sang and danced for the man, and he signed her to a contract at the tender age of twelve. Her father was reluctant to have their child working so hard at such a young age, but mother would not hear him. This was what she had been grooming her girls for, and she made sure the contract was signed. The youngest Garland daughter was bringing in $100 a week, which was more than the family had ever seen.

Soon after, Garland's father died suddenly of spinal meningitis. Garland was devastated by the loss, also realizing that she would have no one to protect her from her increasingly controlling mother. Forced to work long hours by the studio and stressed by the ever-present pushing from her mother, Garland became weak and despondent. The studio's quick fix was to give the youngster amphetamines to keep her awake and energetic during the long hours. There was an extra bonus for the producers in that Garland lost the excess baby fat she carried. The studio doctors also prescribed barbiturates so Garland would be able to sleep at night during filming. During this time, no one saw the long-term effects that this sort of drug usage would cause.

Many years later, Garland would be quoted as saying, "They'd give us pep-up pills to keep us on our feet long after we were exhausted. Then they'd take us to the studio hospital and knock us cold with sleeping pills... Then after four hours, they'd wake us up and give us the pep-up pills again so we could work another seventy-two hours in a row. I started to feel like a wind-up toy from FAO Schwarz."

Garland continued her grueling schedule, but loved working on the lot. In 1938, she was cast in the film "Love Finds Andy Hardy" with costar Mickey Rooney. The high-energy Rooney was the perfect match for her, and the duo would go on to make ten more films together.

The next year, in 1939, the studio was planning a blockbuster film adaptation of the L. Frank Baum book *The Wizard of Oz*. They were in negotiations with 20th Century Fox to borrow mega-star Shirley Temple for the film, but the rival studio would not agree. Garland would inherit the role that would change her life forever and create one of the most beloved characters in the history of film. "Over the Rainbow" became the song audiences would associate with Garland for the rest of her life, but unbeknownst to people outside the production, the song was almost cut from the original film because producers thought it caused the film to drag on too much. At the Academy Awards that year, Garland would be given a special award for her performance in the film.

With the success of Oz under her belt, Garland began working in earnest, making seven films in the next two years. In her next three films, she would be reunited with costar Mickey Rooney for "Babes in Arms," "Andy Hardy Meets a Debutante," and "Strike Up the Band." After that, she was cast in the film "For Me and My Gal," opposite newcomer Gene Kelly.

During this time, Garland was growing up and wanted to take more control of her life. Her mother and the studio would have none of it, so she rebelled in the only way she knew how: she met and married bandleader David Rose, running away to Las Vegas in the summer of 1941 to elope. Rose was twelve years her senior. Soon after the marriage, Garland found out she was pregnant. She was strong-armed into having an abortion by studio executives, who felt having a baby would destroy her image as a wholesome young girl. She reluctantly agreed, but the event would have a lasting effect on her. The marriage also suffered under the constant pressure of her life, and the two divorced in 1945.

Throughout the 1940s, Garland would turn out picture after picture, each film more popular than the last. In 1944, she was offered the role of Rose in the film "Meet Me in St. Louis" with director Vincent Minnelli. She turned the role down, but was talked into making the film, which garnered huge success for her and the studio. During the filming, she became better acquainted with the director, and the two were married. She gave birth to daughter, Liza Minnelli, a year later. Garland went right back to work after the birth, using more drugs to help her cope with postpartum depression and the hectic work schedule. Her behavior became more erratic; physically, she was thin and pale.

She was dropped from the production of "The Barkleys of Broadway" in 1949 for her absences. Later she was also dismissed from "Annie Get Your Gun" and replaced by actress Betty Hutton, who had to redo parts of the film that Garland had already filmed to complete the project.

After her dismissal from the studio, Garland suffered a nervous breakdown and was hospitalized for a short time. She was sent to Boston, Massachusetts, to rest and get clean. She then returned to Hollywood to film "Summer Stock," with her "Get Happy" number from the film gaining critical acclaim. After completing the film, she was offered the lead in "Royal Wedding" with Fred Astaire, after lead actress June Allyson became pregnant. Garland began the project, but collapsed on the set soon after and was replaced by Jane Powell.

In 1951, Garland divorced Minnelli and met her next husband, Sid Luft. She performed for the first time in front of a live audience at the London Palladium that year, enjoying huge success on the stage. She returned to the United States and repeated the performance at the Palace Theater in New York. She continued doing personal appearances and performing. She also gave birth to two more children during her marriage to Luft, who became her manager.

The couple produced "A Star is Born" in 1954, and Garland was nominated for an Academy Award for Best Actress. She went into labor just before the Oscar broadcast and watched from her hospital bed as she lost out to Grace Kelly for her performance in "The Country Girl."

Garland was more distraught than ever. Suffering again from postpartum depression, she was taking more drugs and was unable to find work. In 1959, she hit the bottom when she almost died from complications caused by hepatitis. Several of her close friends thought this was the end of the little girl who became a huge success on the screen, but she would show everyone her resilience two years later, coming back to perform at Carnegie Hall and giving one of the finest performances ever on the stage.

Even with Garland working steadily to packed houses, the Lufts were deeply in debt, owing to their lavish lifestyle and Luft's gambling debts. Garland was offered a television special, followed by a series, "The Judy Garland Show," in 1962. The show proved Garland could still perform vocally, but she struggled to meet the grueling schedule, and the show was canceled after only one season.

Garland and Luft divorced in 1965, both bitterly fighting for custody of their two children. Garland wed young actor Mark Herron, but there was some question as to the legality of the marriage since her divorce from Luft wasn't yet final when they married. That, along with the rumors that the young man was homosexual, led to divorce less than two years later.

In 1967, Garland would be offered parts in both "Harlow" and "Valley of the Dolls," but was let go from both projects. She was being hospitalized more often for rests, and she and her three children were moving often to avoid creditors.

In 1969, Garland married her fifth husband, Mickey Deans, and attempted yet another comeback on the stage. The couple was staying in London while Garland worked out a new nightclub act that she wanted to debut. On June 20, 1969, Garland went to bed after meeting with her press agent. Her husband came to bed sometime around midnight to find her still awake. She had taken a number of sleeping pills already and continued to take more to try to sleep.

The next day, Deans awoke to find Garland absent from the bed. He crossed to the bathroom door and found it locked. He pounded on the door, calling Garland's name, but received no response. Desperate, Deans climbed on the roof and lowered himself to look in the bathroom window. He witnessed Garland sitting on the toilet with her head in her arms, which were resting on her knees. He smashed open the window and lowered himself into the room. He found her unconscious and tried in vain to resuscitate her, but Judy Garland was dead at the age of forty-seven.

An autopsy was scheduled, and the official cause of death was cited as acute barbiturate overdose. Some whispered rumors of suicide, but the coroner ruled out intentional death. Garland's body was flown back to New York and prepared for a lavish funeral.

Judy Garland lay in state wearing a high-collar grey chiffon gown (the same gown she wore at her last wedding) and blanketed with a spray of yellow roses in a white-steel casket. A large rainbow of peonies stood near the casket, a tribute to her song "Over the Rainbow." Dozens of bouquets lined the visitation room from contemporaries like Fred Astaire, Irving Berlin, and Jimmy Stewart.

The visitation was held at the Frank E. Campbell Funeral Home, the same mortuary that had held the funeral for silent-screen actor Rudolph Valentino. An estimated 22,000 fans and admirers filed past the open casket to gaze one last time upon the star who had given them joy on and off the screen. The visitation was to be closed at 11 p.m., but Deans requested that the viewing remain open throughout the night so that the thousands of people crowding the streets could be admitted.

Judy Garland's funeral was held June 27, 1969. Mickey Rooney was asked to give the eulogy, but refused, fearing he would be unable to contain his emotions during the service. James Mason, her co-star in "A Star Is Born," stepped in, later describing the woman this way: "The thing about Judy Garland was that she was so alive. You close your eyes and you see a small, vivid woman—sometimes fat, sometimes thin—but vivid."

The star-studded event was concluded with Garland being interred in a temporary vault at Ferncliff Cemetery in Hartsdale, New York. Her daughter, Liza Minnelli, thought that Deans was to handle the burial arrangements, but he did not have the money to have her buried properly, so Liza had organized the funeral and now was left to deal with raising the money to have her mother's body moved to a large tomb in the mausoleum, which she did a year later.

Deans was asked later why he chose to have Garland buried in New York, to which he replied, "Judy's always wanted to be wherever I am, and my home is here and in London, and I didn't want her where tourist buses and that sort of thing go through."

JAYNE MANSFIELD

Breathy Jayne Mansfield put her mark on Hollywood with her campy wit and forty-inch bust line, but is best remembered for her premature death at age thirty-four.

Mansfield was born into a professional family; her mother was a teacher and her father a lawyer. She lost her father when she was only three years old in a tragic, foreshadowing car accident. She and her mother then moved to Texas, where Mansfield continued her schooling. However, she also had early aspirations of becoming a movie star.

Marrying her high school sweetheart Paul Mansfield at the age of eighteen, she soon gave birth to a daughter, but continued to follow her dreams of stardom. Her husband was called to active duty in the Korean War, and she took the opportunity to pack her bags and take off for California, leaving her young daughter with her mother. She began attending classes at UCLA and entered the Miss California contest. Her husband caught up with her and forced her to drop out of the competition, dragging her back to Texas.

While living in Dallas, she appeared on local television and continued her acting lessons. In 1954, her husband left the military, and the young couple moved to California. Upon their arrival, she put all of her time and energy into getting a studio contract, literally pushing her way into the Paramount Pictures lot, where she was signed almost on sight.

Mansfield made the movie "Female Jungle" for Paramount, but the film was shelved for two years. During this time, her husband was becoming disillusioned with the marriage and decided to return to Texas without his wife. The two divorced in 1958.

Mansfield's press agent, James Byron, made sure that the young starlet received the publicity she craved. No stunt was too ridiculous or revealing for her. She loved showing off her voluptuous body, even posing for a *Playboy* centerfold. She was becoming a hot commodity, and Warner Bros. signed her to a long-term contract.

After appearing in two more films, Mansfield moved to New York to appear in the comedy "Will Success Spoil Rock Hunter?"

The show was a huge success, and she continued pushing for more publicity during the run of the show. It was here that she met future husband Mickey Hargitay, who was performing with Mae West. He left that show to pursue Mansfield, much to the disappointment and anger of West.

Mansfield and Hargitay moved back to Hollywood, where she continued to work hard at keeping herself in the public eye. She appeared in her best film, "The Girl Can't Help It," and followed that success with the film version of "Rock Hunter," recreating the empty-headed blonde character she played on stage. The studio continued to capitalize on Mansfield's successful bimbo stereotype in her next film, "The Wayward Bus."

Mansfield and Hargitay were married January 13, 1958, and had three children together. They lived a lavish lifestyle, purchasing a large, pink, Spanish-style mansion with an outrageous interior, including an all-pink bathroom with a heart-shaped tub. To round out the ostentatious estate, they installed a pink, heart-shaped pool.

The studio sent Mansfield to England, where she starred in several unsuccessful movies, and then moved her to Italy, where she and her husband costarred in "The Loves of Hercules," another flop for Mansfield. Frustrated with her film roles, she continued her outlandish behavior to grab attention, sometimes taking things too far, thus losing her studio contract in the process.

Mansfield took a role in the sleazy sex comedy "Promises Promises" in 1963, desperation starting to force bad decisions. She and Hargitay finally divorced in 1964, causing her to feel more like her life was slipping away. She posed again for *Playboy* and made several more bad pictures before marrying director Matt Cimber. They had a child together, but Mansfield had already begun turning to alcohol to ease her troubled mind.

In 1964, she was offered the role of Ginger in the upcoming new series "Gilligan's Island," but on the advice of her husband, she turned it down, stating, "I am a movie star. I don't do television."

Within two years, her third marriage was over, and she met attorney Samuel Brody and started on a nightclub tour of Europe, which quickly turned into a disaster. Then, briefly, it appeared that Mansfield had turned things around when she toured with Bob Hope, entertaining the troops in Vietnam. Upon her return to the United States, she began her nightclub tour once again, finding herself in Biloxi, Mississippi. After finishing a late show, she and Brody packed her three children, four dogs, and driver Ron Harrison in her Buick Electra for the long ride to New Orleans for her next engagement. Twenty miles outside of New Orleans, a tractor-trailer was stopped on the road, waiting for a city vehicle to finish spraying for mosquitoes. Not seeing the truck, Harrison slammed the car into the back of it, shearing off the top of the car. The three adults in the front were killed instantly. Rumors flew later, saying she was decapitated, but this was not true. The official cause of death was stated as a crushed skull with avulsion of cranium and brain. Mansfield's three children, who had been asleep in the back seat, sustained only minor injuries, but the star was dead at the age of thirty-four.

Mansfield's body was transported back to Hollywood for her memorial service and then shipped to Pennsylvania for burial. The brief funeral was presided over by a local Methodist minister, and she was interred in the family plot in Pen Argyl, Pennsylvania. Twenty years later, the Jayne Mansfield Fan Club purchased a cenotaph and installed it at Hollywood Memorial Park in California. It showed her birth year as 1938 instead of 1933, her actual year of birth.

Jayne Mansfield's estate was valued at $2 million dollars at the time of her death, but after lawyers and creditors drained the assets, each of her children walked away with only $2,000 each.

John Belushi

Considered one of the most talented comedians to come from the original "Saturday Night Live" cast, John Belushi lived his life in high gear and burned out far too early.

The multi-talented Belushi learned early on that he had a gift for making people laugh, being voted class clown and most humorous by his classmates. The homecoming king also excelled at sports, playing football, and he played in a rock band as well.

Being a child of the 1960s, Belushi experimented with marijuana and various other popular drugs. He managed to avoid the draft, being diagnosed with high blood pressure at his exam. What the doctor did not realize is that Belushi had eaten a large amount of salt just prior to the test to elevate his blood pressure. During college, Belushi protested the war in Vietnam and dressed in the hippie garb of the era.

During the summer months, Belushi began acting and soon became the youngest actor in the Second City improvisation group in Chicago, where he perfected his slapstick comedy style and began pursuing a more-active acting career.

In 1973, Belushi was offered a role in the off-Broadway production of "National Lampoon's Lemmings." He received critical acclaim for the role and was offered a position with The National Lampoon's Radio Hour, which he not only performed in, but wrote for as well.

In wasn't until 1975 that Belushi would win the part that would rocket him to fame. Lorne Michaels offered the up-and-coming comedian a part in "Saturday Night Live" in New York. During the next four years, he created memorable characters, including the Samurai Warrior and the Blues Brothers with friend and castmate Dan Aykroyd.

Belushi continued his drug usage, escalating to harder choices like cocaine. His wife, Judy Jacklin, began worrying about her husband. His drug abuse worsened and his job with SNL was threatened on several occasions.

In 1978, he began his movie career, traveling to Mexico to appear in the Robert De Niro production of "Going South." De Niro and Belushi reportedly did not care for each other during the filming, but the experience did not dampen Belushi's desire to continue acting in movies.

The following year, Belushi took a role, along with "Saturday Night Live" pal Dan Aykroyd, in the Steven Spielberg film "1941." While the film did not make money at the box office, Belushi decided it was time to leave television to focus on major motion pictures, and the duo moved forward with their next film, "The Blues Brothers," based on the characters they had developed on SNL. The project was a huge success and re-enforced Belushi's decision to leave television.

Belushi continued to abuse his body with excessive drug use. He became more isolated from his friends and coworkers, not wanting people to see him intoxicated. Even with his personal demons looming daily, he felt it was time to move into a romantic lead role with his next film, "Continental Divide." Critics were less than thrilled with the performances of both lead actors, and the audience stayed away. Belushi finally came to the conclusion that the only way to make a movie in Hollywood was to control the script, so he set out to write his own screenplay.

Later that year, he pitched his new movie "Noble Rot" to Paramount Pictures, but the studio rejected the project, wanting him to film another slapstick comedy, "The Joy of Sex." Belushi, furious by the rejection, returned to the West Coast to rework the script. He left wife Judy behind in New York in order to pursue his goal.

Arriving in Los Angeles, he checked into the Chateau Marmont Hotel on Sunset Boulevard, an exclusive high-end hideaway for celebrities. He was given the key to Bungalow 3 and settled in for a weekend of nonstop partying and drug use.

On March 4, 1982, Belushi went to a local nightclub with some friends and drank heavily in addition to taking several drugs. He returned to the hotel alone, but soon called known drug dealer Catherine Evelyn Smith to join him. Belushi was looking pale, but continued his binge, mixing cocaine and alcohol. Smith introduced Belushi to "speed balls," a mixture of cocaine and heroin. Resisting the need to rest, Belushi continued partying with friends Robin Williams and Robert De Niro into the early hours on March 5.

Later that morning, Belushi showered and went to bed. Smith gave him one more injection of the lethal drug mixture and left the star alone to get some rest. About an hour later, Belushi awoke, having trouble breathing. Smith came into the room to check on her new friend, and he insisted that he was fine, lying back down. Smith checked on him one more time around 10:15 a.m. before leaving the room to run a personal errand.

At noon, Belushi's physical therapist, William Wallace, arrived at the hotel for a previously planned workout session. Entering the room, he found Belushi lying on the bed on his side. The room seemed eerily quiet, with no sounds of snoring or breathing coming from his client. He checked for a pulse and called the front desk, asking for an ambulance. Wallace desperately tried to revive Belushi until the paramedics arrived fifteen minutes later. Belushi was pronounced dead at the scene. A call was made to Dan Aykroyd, telling him of his friend's passing. Aykroyd went to Belushi's house to tell his wife personally of her husband's death. An autopsy revealed that Belushi died of acute cocaine and heroin intoxication.

John Belushi's body was flown back to New York, and the funeral was scheduled for March 8, 1982. The service was attended by close family and friends at Abel's Hill Cemetery in Martha's Vineyard. Dan Aykroyd led the procession on his motorcycle, clad in blue jeans and a black leather jacket. James Taylor sang at the gravesite while friends wept openly. A second public memorial service was scheduled for March 11 at the Cathedral of Saint John the Divine, attended by all of Belushi's friends and contemporaries.

Soon after Belushi's death, his widow requested an investigation of her husband's death and the involvement of Cathy Smith. In March 1983, a grand jury determined that Smith's actions were negligent and scheduled a trial. In June 1986, Smith pleaded guilty to involuntary manslaughter in an attempt to avoid murder charges. She received a sentence of ten years for her contribution to the death of one of Hollywood's best-loved funnymen (but served only eighteen months).

Several years later, Belushi's widow felt compelled to move his body from the original gravesite. Scores of fans came to the small cemetery in Martha's Vineyard, vandalizing other gravesites in the process. Belushi is now in an unmarked grave, but loyal followers continue to leave tokens of love at the original gravesite since the current grave is unknown.

CHRIS FARLEY

Another of the "Saturday Night Live" cast to live his life in excess was Chris Farley, known for his manic, high-volume brand of comedy. Farley's life and death proved to be all too similar to that of actor — and Farley idol — John Belushi.

As a child, Farley suffered from weight problems and found approval with his peers by being a class clown and insulting himself before others could ridicule him. The nuns at the Catholic school he attended did not find his antics funny, though he continued cutting up with his friends throughout high school, constantly looking to be the center of attention.

Farley decided to pursue his acting seriously and was accepted to Marquette University in Milwaukee, Wisconsin, a Jesuit/Roman Catholic university. Even with his affinity for comedy, Farley was deeply religious and a devout Catholic.

After graduating in 1987, Farley moved to Chicago and joined the Improv Olympic theater, a precursor to the Second City troupe of performers. Within one year, he was accepted to Second City and continued to perfect his over-the-top physical comedy. For the next two years, he enjoyed great success and began a life of excess that would haunt him for the rest of his days.

At the end of 1989, Lorne Michaels invited Farley to join the cast of "Saturday Night Live." Excited to follow in the footsteps of his idol John Belushi, Farley jumped at the chance. He enjoyed creating several outrageous characters on the show, each more obnoxious and physically humorous than the last. One of his favorite pranks involved dropping his pants in front of the cast and audience at unsuspecting moments.

While Farley's success skyrocketed, so did his lust for excess. He began taking drugs, drinking, eating, and having sex at an alarming rate. His substance abuse became so severe that producers warned him to get clean or lose his job.

Farley took steps to get clean and performed volunteer work with senior citizens at a local church. His white-knuckle approach to sobriety was doomed to fail, and he soon found himself riding high with his addictions. Costar and friend Tom Arnold intervened, convincing him to enter rehab once again before Lorne Michaels could fire the actor.

While his addiction to drugs seemed to be under control, Farley continued to indulge in his other vices. However, others expressed little concern for Farley during this time since his work was not being affected.

In 1992, Farley was offered his first role in a movie. Playing bit parts in comedies such as "Wayne's World," "Coneheads," and "Airheads," he continued sobriety and moved into leading roles. In 1994, he left the cast of SNL to pursue his film career in earnest. His first film, "Tommy Boy," in which he partnered with funnyman David Spade, had moderate success at the box office, and Farley received $2 million dollars for the effort. Seeing chemistry between the two actors, the studio continued pairing them in "Black Sheep" and "Beverley Hills Ninja," and Farley earned $6 million for his role in Ninja.

Though his career was on a high, Farley continued to struggle with abstaining from drugs. He continued to attend church regularly, seeking prayers and assistance from his priest, but was unable to find the strength to stay clean. Farley continued serving others in the community with donations of his time and resources, but his life spun out of control once again.

In 1997, Farley was asked to come back to SNL, this time as host. His appearance shocked some of the performers, and there was great concern that he might not be able to complete the filming. At the urging of friends and colleagues, he went back to Chicago to enter rehab once again, but failed to complete the program. Upon leaving the center, Farley pushed the envelope, continuing to abuse his body with drugs, alcohol, food, and sex. Now weighing over three hundred pounds, Farley knew he had to get sober before his next movie began filming the next month.

On December 11, 1997, he went to one of his favorite local pubs and drank excessively. He continued his binge throughout the weekend, but was rumored to be able to attend church that Sunday. Gorging himself on food and booze Sunday night, he finally returned home, where he continued using drugs. Farley contacted a local exotic dancer to come to his home for a private show. Later, the dancer confessed to only dancing for the star and leaving immediately after she finished.

Farley continued his party with friends the next day into the pre-dawn hours, finally taking the party to the home of a friend in Lincoln Park. Cocaine, heroin, and liquor were plentiful at the party, and Farley invited several strippers to join the fun, eventually leaving with one of the girls. He went to her apartment, and the two continued doing drugs and drinking. He later called a limousine to take them back to his home for the night.

At 3 a.m. on December 18, Farley's companion was ready to go, but he begged her not to leave him alone. Suddenly, Farley collapsed on the floor, but the girl testified later she thought it was a joke and snapped a picture of him to share with him later.

In the early afternoon, Farley's brother arrived at the apartment to visit and found him unconscious on the floor. Investigators determined that the young comedian had been dead several hours prior to his brother arriving on the scene. An autopsy later found lethal doses of cocaine and heroin in his system.

On December 23, 1997, family and friends gathered at Our Lady Queen of Peace Catholic Church in Chicago to say farewell to their friend. Farley's aunt and uncle both read scripture during the service and long-time friend and schoolmate Matthew Foley gave the homily. Farley's brother read the poem "A Clown's Prayer," which was also printed in the program. Longtime friend Tom Arnold gave the eulogy, and the service concluded with a soloist singing "When Irish Eyes Are Smiling." Chris Farley's casket was carried to Resurrection Cemetery, where he was laid to rest.

A second, public service was held in California on January 12, 1998, to honor the actor. Noticeably absent from both services was costar David Spade. He was later quoted as saying he "could not be in a room where Chris was in a box."

SAM COOKE

Said to be one of the inventors of soul music, Sam Cooke was taken from legions of adoring fans at the pinnacle of his success. Anyone within earshot of Cooke while he sang as a boy knew he had a gift. Performing in church from a young age, he was said to bring people from far and near to hear his voice lifted in song.

It was when Cooke was offered to front the gospel singing group The Soul Stirrers that he skyrocketed to success, traveling across the United States for the next six years. Witnessing the treatment of black people during his travels, Cooke became an advocate for civil rights and refused to sing in segregated concerts, branding himself as a radical with his civil disobedience.

Feeling ready to move his career forward, Cooke decided to record a soul/rhythm and blues album against the advice of friends. Cooke's first single, "You Send Me," became an instant success, selling over one million copies alone. Being romanced by several record companies, he signed with RCA records as the first major black performer. Not long after, he became disillusioned with the deal and created his own record company, allowing him to control his music and publishing rights. Cooke was the first performer of any color to take full control of his business in this way.

Gravesite of Sam Cooke in private garden at Forest Lawn Memorial Park Glendale, California.

Cooke continued having great success musically, hitting his pinnacle with the 1962 album Night Beat. While he was enjoying a happy professional career, tragedy struck his family with the death of his infant son. Cooke sank into a deep depression, not working for most of 1963. Even with his self-imposed isolation, he continued making more money than any black performer of the time, and his business affairs remained secure.

On the evening of December 10, 1964, Cooke went to a favorite restaurant, where he met Elisa Boyer, a known prostitute. The two went to P.J.'s nightclub, drinking and listening to music until after midnight, and then drove to the Hacienda Motel in El Segundo California, where they spent several hours together. Sometime during the interlude, Cooke went to the bathroom and Boyer left the room with over $5,000 in cash she found in Cooke's wallet. She went to the manager's office, the two women having collaborated in the swindle.

Upon realizing that he had been robbed, Cooke rushed to the manager's office to report the theft, only to find the two women counting the money while he looked on through the window. Clad only in a sport coat and shoes and naked from the waist down, he burst into the office and startled the two accomplices. Bertha Franklin, the manager, shot Cooke at pointblank range, killing the singer.

After the shooting, Boyer went to a pay phone and called police, claiming she was kidnapped by Cooke and forced into the hotel room. She then claimed that she had escaped when Cooke went to the restroom, and in scooping up her discarded clothing, she had accidentally taken some of Cooke's belongings in her haste to escape. She quickly donned her clothing and discarded the other items while attempting to find help. When asked why she did not go to the manager's office, she alleged that she knocked on the door, but the manager took too long to answer and she feared Cooke would come after her.

The story from Bertha Franklin had Cooke coming to the office demanding to know the whereabouts of Boyer. When Franklin told him she did not know, he became enraged, attacking the woman. A struggle ensued and they fell to the ground, but Franklin was able to get up and retrieve her gun, shooting the man in self-defense.

Questions surrounded the investigation of the death. The coroner's report glaringly ignored the body's severe bruising on the head and arms, the face so badly beaten that he was almost unrecognizable to investigators. Also ignored was the whereabouts of the clothing, the money, and the wallet Boyer took... the items seemed to disappear. Cooke's family continues to believe in a conspiracy to hide evidence as to the facts concerning the events of that fateful night.

After an autopsy was performed, Sam Cooke's body was flown to Chicago, Illinois, where Cooke's wife arranged a grand funeral in his favorite city. Cooke was laid out in a grey suit, and he appeared at peace in the open casket, despite his face and hands still showing signs of the beating he endured.

Lou Rawls and The Staples Singers sang for their lost friend and hundreds of admirers filled the church to say goodbye to a music legend. A second service was held in California, with Ray Charles performing a musical tribute. Sam Cooke was laid to rest at Forest Lawn in Glendale, California in a private garden, accessible only by family members who were given the key to the large bronze door.

Chapter Six:

THE FINAL RESTING PLACES

Cemeteries are not just for dead people anymore. Nowhere is this fact found to be true more than in Hollywood, where people by the dozens excitedly tour these once sacred places.

What intrigues us about the final resting places of our favorite celebrities? Why do people flock to the Los Angeles area and beyond to seek out and get as close as possible to movie stars? Ask why busloads of tourists buy maps to the movie stars homes or famous restaurants where they once ate?

Cemeteries have many reproductions of famous artwork, including Da Vinci's "Last Supper," recreated in stained glass, at Forest Lawn Memorial Park Glendale.

The famous "Hollywood" sign as seen from the grounds of Hollywood Forever.

As a culture, we are mesmerized by the lives, and more so, by the deaths of these icons of the silver screen. I have watched on a clear, sunny Saturday in June as tourists armed with maps, books, and printed directions storm the gates of these cemeteries to touch the cold, hard marble crypt front of Dean Martin, place flowers at the headstone of Bing Crosby, or sit and have lunch with Rita Hayworth. It may seem macabre to some, but I have seen firsthand the rising numbers of travelers who make visiting these destinations a part of their vacation travel plans.

Sometimes the cemeteries themselves can have a past just as torrid as the lives of the movies stars who inhabit these gardens. Included in this chapter are the most prominent graveyards and a who's who of the people who broke ground on their last locations.

Forest Lawn Memorial Park

1712 South Glendale Avenue, Glendale, California

The cemetery known as Forest Lawn Memorial Park in Glendale, California, started its life as a small, dreary, run of the mill non-profit cemetery in 1906. Ten years later this area, then known as Tropico, California, hired a young Robert Eaton to sell plots in a small, cramped shack on the twelve-acre property.

Rumor has it that on New Year Day 1917, Robert stood overlooking the acreage and decided then to purchase the land to create a memorial park that would create sunshine instead of darkness, thus a new era of cemetery was born. Robert stated publicly he wanted to celebrate life with rolling gardens and stately monuments. Included in his plan was statuary and grand mausoleums in a three hundred-acre space, with room for 300,000 loved ones.

Some claim Robert was a visionary while others say he was an opportunist who wanted to create a monopoly on the burgeoning Los Angeles area and create his own empire. In 1934, Robert Eaton opened the first mortuary on cemetery grounds; this full service mortuary/cemetery combination allowed the public to choose funeral arrangements and burial all at one time in a one-stop shop for all your funeral needs.

Over 1,500 monuments are scattered throughout the sprawling property. A good number of those are reproductions of great works of art by the most famous artisans

The "Great Mausoleum" at dusk. Forest Lawn Memorial Park in Glendale, California.

throughout history. Within the walls of the Great Mausoleum stands Leonardo Da Vinci's "Last Supper," recreated in stained glass.

With the beauty and serenity of this place, it is no wonder that some of the greatest Hollywood stars would choose Forest Lawn as their final residence.

View of the Great Mausoleum from "L. Frank Baum" tomb in Forest Lawn Memorial Park, Glendale, California.

While the cemetery staff is instructed not to give out the grave locations of these stars, I have spent the better part of my life hunting down these greats with the help of other grave hunting enthusiasts. Within the Great Mausoleum are the final homes to actor Clark Gable and his wife Carole Lombard, comedians Red Skelton and W. C. Fields, famed theater owner Sid Grauman, silent film actress Theda Bara, and man of a thousand faces Lon Chaney.

In the Freedom Mausoleum are favorites like funny man George Burns, his wife Gracie Allen, actress/singer Jeanette MacDonald,

Celtic Cross headstone with Great Mausoleum in background at Forest Lawn Memorial Park in Glendale, California.

crooner Nat "King" Cole, silent film stars Clara Bow and Rex Bell, actress Dorothy Dandridge, the Three Stooges' Larry Fine, Marx Brother Gummo Marx, actor/comedians Billy Barty and Francis X. Bushman, and Western film star Alan Ladd.

Some of our favorite stars decided on more traditional burials such as actor Jimmy Stewart, singer/dancer Sammy Davis Jr., America's sweetheart Mary Pickford, swashbuckler Errol Flynn, actor Spencer Tracy, *Wizard of Oz* author L. Frank Baum, actor Ted Knight, actor Humphrey Bogart, and director Vincent Minnelli.

FOREST LAWN HOLLYWOOD HILLS

6300 Forest Lawn Drive, Los Angeles, California

On the east end of the Santa Monica Mountains stands a four hundred-acre memorial park known as Forest Lawn Memorial Park Hollywood Hills. This cemetery stands in the middle of the thriving film and television Mecca of Los Angeles and hosts many of the most famous stars in Hollywood.

Opened in 1948, this memorial park is quite different from its predecessor in Glendale. Forest Lawn Hollywood Hills was built to remind us of our United States history with full-scale reproductions of the Old North Church and a sprawling mosaic of the country's history.

As you enter the gates of this cemetery, you will find the famous cowboy Gene Autry and his sidekick Smiley Burnette, Walt Disney's brother Roy Disney, actor Jack Webb, and actress Dorothy La'Mour.

In the grand outdoor mausoleum is famed actress Bette Davis, pianist Liberace, comedian Freddy Prinze, Sr., lion tamer Clyde Beatty, singers Andy Gibb and Lou Rawls, teen idol Sandra Dee, and television funnyman Morey Amsterdam.

In the celebrated Washington memorial section are comedians Marty Feldman, Buster Keaton, Stan Laurel, and John Ritter, TV tough guy Telly Savalas, talk show host Steve Allen, the Scatman Crothers, and Batman™ Bob Cane.

PIERCE BROTHERS WESTWOOD MEMORIAL PARK

1218 Glendon Avenue,
Los Angeles, California

Tucked away between the huge structures of downtown Los Angeles, California, lays a hidden treasure of the Hollywood elite. Pierce Brothers Westwood Memorial Park opened in 1904 as a much larger cemetery than the small two-acre plot of ground you see now. The owners sold off large sections of the cemetery grounds in 1927 to developers, but kept the quiet peacefulness of the small cemetery amidst the explosive growth around them.

This small memorial park would have remained unknown if not for the burial of Marilyn Monroe in 1962. Monroe visited Westwood quite often after the passing of Grace Goddard, a family friend and Monroe's caretaker as a child. Now, decades later, this cemetery has become one of the highly sought after burial places for the Hollywood A-list celebrities.

In addition to Marilyn Monroe, Westwood is home to comedians like Don Knotts, Eddie Albert, Jim Backus, and Rodney Dangerfield. Talk show host Merv Griffin, 1970s actress and pin-up Farrah Fawcett, and acclaimed actors Walter Matthau and George C. Scott also have chosen Westwood as their final resting place.

Musicians Frank Zappa, Carl Wilson, Dean Martin, and Roy Orbison are laid to rest in the center lawn, with actress Natalie Wood, Hogan's Heroes actor Bob Crane, and leading man Burt Lancaster close by in this same section.

Other burials at Westwood include pin-up queen Betty Page, All in the Family actor Carroll O'Connor, funnyman Jack Lemmon, writer/director Billy Wilder, writer Truman Capote, and crooner Mel Torme.

"Green Acres" actress Eva Gabor is tucked away in a quiet corner of the cemetery with actor John Cassavettes, and "Poltergeist" actress Heather O'Rourke is buried here along with on-screen sister Dominique Dunne.

For such a small cemetery well hidden by the towering skyscrapers surrounding the quiet garden, Westwood is one of the best known for the bevy of Hollywood stars within its walls.

HOLLYWOOD FOREVER CEMETERY

6000 Santa Monica Boulevard, Los Angeles, California

One of the oldest cemeteries in Los Angeles is the famed Hollywood Forever cemetery on Santa Monica Boulevard. Once known as Hollywood Memorial Park, it opened its gates in 1899, just a few years after Hollywood was established and long before the movie industry would come to the West Coast. Originally opened with one hundred acres, this cemetery's history is like something you would read in a movie script or see on the screen.

It was at the turn-of-the-century that cemeteries became money-making ventures for the owners instead of non-profit organizations run by churches and some of the townsfolk felt this was a hindrance to civic progress and the welfare of the community. Thus a group formed and issued a formal complaint to the city council to have Hollywood Memorial Park shut down. The city council found in favor of the cemetery, but their problems would continue.

By the 1920s, Hollywood Memorial Park became the place of celebrity burials. Tourists visited the grounds regularly, seeking their favorite silent film actors. By the 1940s, the Forest Lawn Company was beginning to take quite a percentage of the elite burial business and Hollywood Memorial Park was suffering once again.

With new management at the helm and no one watching, the endowment funds began to disappear and by 1990, the park was in complete disrepair. An investigation found that millions of dollars had been stolen and the cemetery was forced to file for bankruptcy. The cemetery association put the historical cemetery up for sale with a price tag of $375,000. Luckily, Forever Industries purchased the land and immediately went to work restoring the grounds to their former splendor. Now Hollywood Forever is home to celebrities, past and present, and will continue for generations to come.

Some of the notable burials within these walls are Douglas Fairbanks Jr. and Sr., "King Kong" actress Fay Wray, actor Tyrone Powers, and famed actress Marion Davies.

Temple Beth Olam mausoleum. Hollywood Forever Cemetery in Hollywood, California.

The Clarke Mausoleum at Hollywood Forever Cemetery in Hollywood, California.

Overview of the Garden of Legends at Hollywood Forever Cemetery in Hollywood, California.

Tyrone Powers' headstone with the Cathedral Mausoleum in the background at Hollywood Forever Cemetery in Hollywood, California.

A view of the corridor of the Cathedral Mausoleum at Hollywood Forever Cemetery in Hollywood, California.

Some infamous burials include Jayne Mansfield's cenotaph, gangster Bugsy Siegel, and starlet Virginia Rappe. Dancer Eleanor Powell resides within the Cathedral Mausoleum along with Peter Lorre, William Desmond Taylor, and Peter Finch.

In the Abbey of the Psalms Mausoleum stands crypts for Our Gang alumnus Darla Hood, Clifton Webb, and producer Jesse Lasky. Indian actor Iron Eyes Cody, actress Joan Hackett, and actress Norma Talmadge are also in this section.

Some of the celebrities to grace the garden surrounding the large lake are musicians Joey Ramone and brother Dee Dee Ramone, "Get Smart" actor Don Adams, director John Huston, and producer and studio head Cecil B. DeMille.

Animator/voice-over artist Mel Blanc resides at Hollywood Forever with Our Gang's Alfalfa Carl Switzer and "The Golden Girls" actress Estelle Getty.

"THAT'S ALL FOLKS"
MEL BLANC
MAN OF 1000 VOICES
BELOVED HUSBAND AND FATHER
1908 — 1989

The great voice animator Mel Blanc is among the many performing artists buried at the Hollywood Forever Cemetery.

Holy Cross Cemetery

5835 West Slauson Avenue, Culver City, California

Opened in 1939, Holy Cross Catholic Cemetery is host to many of Hollywood favorite stars from the stage and screen.

One of the most celebrated sections of this large cemetery is the Grotto section, a small plot of land with the likes of Bing Crosby, "Wizard of Oz" actor Jack Haley, comedian Zazu Pitts, French actor Charles Boyer, "Dracula" star Bela Lugosi, and actress Sharon Tate, who is, unfortunately, best known as a victim of the Charles Manson murders.

Nearby is funnyman Jimmy Durante, dancer Ann Miller, child actor Jackie Coogan, and Los Angeles Lakers announcer Chick Hearn.

Located in the mausoleum at the center of the park is comedic actor John Candy, actor Fred MacMurray, comic musician Spike Jones, studio head Eddie Mannix and his wife Toni, musician Jose Iturbi, and dancer Ray Bolger.

Across the lawns are bandleader Lawrence Welk, "Newhart" actress Mary Frann, and Dennis Day.

The Grotto at Holy Cross Cemetery in Culver City, California.

HILLSIDE MEMORIAL PARK

6001 West Centinela Avenue, Los Angeles, California

Opening in 1941 after ten of the Los Angeles Jewish community leaders purchased forty acres of property to use as a cemetery, within the next five years, Hillside was a fully operating cemetery.

One of the most prominent residents is singer Al Jolson. As you enter the gates of Hillside Memorial Park, to your right is a ten-story waterfall with a marble gazebo atop the structure. If you stand at the top of the falls, you will see the large black marble tomb of Jolson and a bronze statue of the actor/singer/dancer in his classic "Mammy" pose.

Neighboring Jolson are actress Suzanne Pleshette, actor Tom Poston, and actress Shelley Winters.

In the nearby mausoleum, "The Fugitive" star David Janssen, Americas Toastmaster General George Jessel, "Bonanza" and "Little House on the Prairie" star Michael Landon, The Max Factor cosmetics family dynasty, and singer/talk show host Dinah Shore. Funnyman Eddie Cantor and the great comedian Jack Benny reside within these walls in a magnificent black marble crypt. Not to be outdone is television producer Aaron Spelling in a white marble crypt; Spelling being one of the newest interments to the cemetery.

In addition to these great performers is "Bonanza" actor Lorne Green, animator "Fritz" Freleng of Warner Brothers fame, "Three Stooges" leader Moe Howard, Milton "Uncle Milty" Berle, and the singer/actress Nell Carter.

CALVARY CEMETERY

4201 Whittier Boulevard, Los Angeles, California

Originally one of the first cemeteries in Los Angeles, California, Calvary Cemetery opened in 1844. Blessed by the parish priest in November of that year, it would be twenty-two years later until Bishop Thaddeus Amat officially consecrated the ground. In that same year, the cemetery had its only real scandal when someone in the area broke open the gates and buried a body illegally on the grounds — the only case of this kind in Los Angeles history.

The cemetery quickly filled and was closed to burials in 1896. A new cemetery was built and the old Calvary Cemetery was quickly forgotten, left to neglect and ruin. Finally in 1925 the city passed an ordinance to move all the bodies out of the old property and this was completed in only five years.

The new cemetery boasts an enormous white facade mausoleum with many alcoves for private family burials. Within the building stands a Catholic chapel at the top of the ornate marble stairs. Here, most of the most well-known celebrities have been placed. Acting dynasty John, Lionel, and Ethel Barrymore are interred here. Years later brother John was disinterred by his grandson and cremated. His remains were then reburied in

This is the front of the Mausoleum at Calvary Cemetery in Los Angeles.

Philadelphia's Mt. Vernon Cemetery. The crypt still remains empty with the nameplate of John Barrymore remaining.

The infant son of Lou Costello is also interred here with his father and mother, dying in an accidental drowning at the age of one. Singer/Actress Irene Dunne resides nearby, along with Polish silent star Pola Negri and comic actress Mabel Normand.

Buried on the ground at Calvary are the parents of former actor/president Ronald Reagan, John and Nelle, former leader of "The Three Stooges" Ted Healy, actor Ramon Novarro, and actress Dolores Costello Barrymore, best known for being the former wife of John Barrymore.

Bibliography

Books

Basten, Fred E. and Paddy Calistro. *The Hollywood Archive: The Hidden History of Hollywood in the Golden Age*. New York, New York: Universe Publishing, 2000.

Burk, Margaret. *Final Curtain*. Santa Ana, California: Seven Locks Press, 1996.

Clarke, Gerald. *Get Happy: The Life of Judy Garland*. New York, New York: Random House, 2000.

CUT! Hollywood Murders, Accidents and Other Tragedies. Lane Cove, Australia: Global Book Publishing, 2005.

Fleming, E. J. *Hollywood Death and Scandal Sites*. Jefferson, North Carolina: McFarland, 2000.

Holden, Anthony. *Behind the Oscar: The Secret History of the Academy Awards*. New York, New York: Plume Publishers, 1993.

Kirkpatrick, Sidney D. *A Cast of Killers*. New York, New York: E.P. Dutton, 1986.

Largo, Michael. *Final Exits: The Illustrated Encyclopedia of How We Die*. New York, New York: HarperCollins Publishers, 2006.

Leider, Emily Worth. *Dark Lover: The Life and Death of Rudolph Valentino*. United Kingdom (London): Faber and Faber, 2004.

Luft, Lorna. *Me and My Shadows: A Family Memoir*. Australia: Pocket Books, 1999.

Masek, Mark. *Hollywood Remains to Be Seen*. Nashville, Tennessee: Cumberland House, 2001.

Miller, David. *Ripley's Believe It or Not! Encyclopedia of the Bizarre: Amazing, Strange, Inexplicable, Weird and All True*. New York, New York: Black Dog & Leventhal, 2005.

Orloff, Erica and Joann Baker. *The Big Sleep: True Tale and Twisted Trivia about Death*. New York, New York: Random House, 1998.

Panati, Charles. *Panati's Extraordinary Endings of Practically Everything and Everybody*. New York, New York: Harper & Row Publishers, 1989.

Parish, James Robert. *Hollywood Book of Death*. New York, New York: McGraw Hill, 2002.

Sheinwold, Patricia Fox. *Too Young to Die*. Baltimore, Maryland: Ottenheimer Publishers Inc., 1979.

Zollo, Paul. *Hollywood Remembered: An Oral History of Its Golden Age*. New York, New York: Cooper Square Press, 2002.

At Hollywood Forever, "Gone With the Wind" actress Hattie McDaniel's memorial is shown with the Clarke mausoleum in the background. McDaniel won Best Supporting Actress for her work in "Gone With the Wind" — the first African American woman to win an Oscar.

FILM AND TELEVISION

A&E Biography
E! Entertainment True Hollywood Story
Elvis Presley: The Last 24 hours
Hollywood Biographies: The Leading Ladies
Hollywood Biographies: The Leading Men
Life with Judy Garland: Me and My Shadows.
Jonestown: the Life of People's Temple

WEBSITES

http://www.barbaralamarr.com
http://www.biography.com
http://www.classichollywoodbios.com
http://www.crimemagazine.com/Celebrities
http://www.Hollywoodgravehunter.com
http://www.IMDB.com
http://www.jimnolt.com/cal.htm
http://www.rudolph-valentino.com
http://www.silentladies.com
http://www.silent-movies.com
http://www.thehollywoodsigngirl.com
http://www.time.com/time/magazine/article/0,9171,744399-2,00.html
http://www.trutv.com/library/crime/notorious_murders/celebrity/sam_cooke/10.
    html
http://www.vh1.com/artists/az/cooke_sam/bio.jhtmlv

INDEX